PROPERTIES OF ECOSYSTEMS

TEACHER SUPPLEMENT

1:1
answersingenesis
Petersburg, Kentucky, USA

ANSWERS IN GENESIS SCIENCE BY DEBBIE & RICHARD LAWRENCE

God's Design for Chemistry & Ecology
Properties of Ecosystems Teacher Supplement

Second printing January 2012

Published by Answers in Genesis, 2800 Bullittsburg Church Rd., Petersburg KY 41080

You may contact the authors at (970) 686-5744

ISBN: 1-60092-286-4

Cover design & layout: Diane King
Editors: Lori Jaworski, Gary Vaterlaus

The publisher and authors have made every reasonable effort to ensure that the activities recommended in this book are safe when performed as instructed but assume no responsibility for any damage caused or sustained while conducting the experiments and activities. It is the parents', guardians', and/or teachers' responsibility to supervise all recommended activities.

Printed in China

www.answersingenesis.org www.godsdesignscience.com

Table of Contents

Welcome to
God's Design® for Chemistry & Ecology

God's Design for Chemistry & Ecology is a series that has been designed for use in teaching chemistry and ecology to elementary and middle school students. It is divided into three books: *Properties of Matter*, *Properties of Atoms and Molecules*, and *Properties of Ecosystems.* Each book has 35 lessons including a final project that ties all of the lessons together.

In addition to the lessons, special features in each book include biographical information on interesting people as well as fun facts to make the subject more fun.

Although this is a complete curriculum, the information included here is just a beginning, so please feel free to add to each lesson as you see fit. A resource guide is included in the appendices to help you find additional information and resources. A list of supplies needed is included at the beginning of each lesson, while a master list of all supplies needed for the entire series can be found in the appendices.

Answer keys for all review questions, worksheets, quizzes, and the final exam are included here. Reproducible student worksheets and tests may be found on the supplementary CD-Rom for easy printing. Please contact Answers in Genesis if you wish to purchase a printed version of all the student materials, or go to www.AnswersBookstore.com.

If you wish to get through all three books in the *Chemistry & Ecology* series in one year, you should plan on covering approximately three lessons per week. The time required for each lesson varies depending on how much additional information you want to include, but you can plan on about 45 minutes per lesson.

If you wish to cover the material in more depth, you may add additional information and take a longer period of time to cover all the material or you could choose to do only one or two of the books in the series as a unit study.

Why Teach Chemistry & Ecology?

Maybe you hate science or you just hate teaching it. Maybe you love science but don't quite know how to teach it to your children. Maybe science just doesn't seem as important as some of those other subjects you need to teach. Maybe you need a little motivation. If any of these descriptions fits you, then please consider the following.

It is not uncommon to question the need to teach your kids hands-on science in elementary school. We could argue that the knowledge gained in science will be needed later in life in order for your children to be more productive and well-rounded adults. We could argue that teaching your children science also teaches them logical and inductive thinking and reasoning skills, which are tools they will need to be more successful. We could argue that science is a necessity in this technological world in which we live. While all of these arguments are true, not one of them is the real reason that we should teach our children science. The most important reason to teach science in elementary school is to give your children an understanding that God is our Creator, and the Bible can be trusted. Teaching science from a creation perspective is one of the best ways to reinforce your children's faith in God and to help them counter the evolutionary propaganda they face every day.

God is the Master Creator of everything. His handiwork is all around us. Our Great Creator put in place all of the laws of physics, biology, and chemistry. These laws were put here for us to see His wisdom and power. In science, we see the hand of God at work more than in any other subject. Romans 1:20 says, "For since the creation of the world His invisible attributes are clearly seen, being understood by the things that are made, even His eternal power and Godhead, so that they [men] are without excuse." We need to help our children see God as Creator of the world around them so they will be able to recognize God and follow Him.

The study of chemistry helps us understand and appreciate the amazing way everything God created works together. The study of atoms and molecules and how different substances react with each other reveals an amazing design, even at the smallest level of life. Understanding the carbon, nitrogen, and water cycles helps our children see that God has a plan to keep everything working together. Learning about ecosystems reveals God's genius in nature.

It's fun to teach chemistry and ecology! It's interesting too. The elements of chemistry are all around us. Children naturally like to combine things to see what will happen. You just need to direct their curiosity.

Finally, teaching chemistry is easy. You won't have to try to find strange materials for experiments or do dangerous things to learn about chemistry. Chemistry is as close as your kitchen or your own body, and ecosystems are just outside your door.

How Do I Teach Science?

In order to teach any subject, you need to understand that people learn in different ways. Most people, and children in particular, have a dominant or preferred learning style in which they absorb and retain information more easily.

If a student's dominant style is:

Auditory
He needs not only to hear the information but he needs to hear himself say it. This child needs oral presentation as well as oral drill and repetition.

Visual
She needs things she can see. This child responds well to flashcards, pictures, charts, models, etc.

Kinesthetic
He needs active participation. This child remembers best through games, hands-on activities, experiments, and field trips.

Also, some people are more relational while others are more analytical. The relational student needs to know why this subject is important and how it will affect him personally. The analytical student, however, wants just the facts.

If you are trying to teach more than one student, you will probably have to deal with more than one learning style. Therefore, you need to present your lessons in several different ways so that each student can grasp and retain the information.

Grades 3–8

Each lesson should be completed by all upper elementary and junior high students. This is the main part of the lesson containing a reading section, a hands-on activity that reinforces the ideas in the reading section (blue box), and a review section that provides review questions and application questions (red box).

Grades 6–8

For middle school/junior high age students, we provide a "Challenge" section that contains more challenging material as well as additional activities and projects for older students (green box).

We suggest a threefold approach to each lesson:

Introduce the topic

We give a brief description of the facts. Frequently you will want to add more information than the essentials given in this book. In addition to reading this section aloud, you may wish to do one or more of the following:

- Read a related book with your students.
- Write things down to help your visual students.
- Give some history of the subject. We provide some historical sketches to help you, but you may want to add more.
- Ask questions to get your students thinking about the subject.

Make observations and do experiments

- Hands-on projects are suggested for each lesson. This section of each lesson may require help from the teacher.
- Have your students perform the activity by themselves whenever possible.

Review

- The "What did we learn?" section has review questions.
- The "Taking it further" section encourages students to
  - Draw conclusions
  - Make applications of what was learned
  - Add extended information to what was covered in the lesson
- The "FUN FACT" section adds fun or interesting information.

By teaching all three parts of the lesson, you will be presenting the material in a way that all learning styles can both relate to and remember.

Also, this approach relates directly to the scientific method and will help your students think more scientifically. The *scientific method* is just a way to examine a subject logically and learn from it. Briefly, the steps of the scientific method are:

1. Learn about a topic.
2. Ask a question.
3. Make a hypothesis (a good guess).
4. Design an experiment to test your hypothesis.
5. Observe the experiment and collect data.
6. Draw conclusions. (Does the data support your hypothesis?)

Note: It's okay to have a "wrong hypothesis." That's how we learn. Be sure to help your students understand why they sometimes get a different result than expected.

Our lessons will help your students begin to approach problems in a logical, scientific way.

How Do I Teach Creation vs. Evolution?

We are constantly bombarded by evolutionary ideas about the earth in books, movies, museums, and even commercials. These raise many questions: Is a living being just a collection of chemicals? Did life begin as a random combination of chemicals? Can life be recreated in a laboratory? What does the chemical evidence tell us about the earth? The Bible answers these questions, and this book accepts the historical accuracy of the Bible as written. We believe this is the only way we can teach our children to trust that everything God says is true.

There are five common views of the origins of life and the age of the earth:

Historical biblical account	Progressive creation	Gap theory	Theistic evolution	Naturalistic evolution
Each day of creation in Genesis is a normal day of about 24 hours in length, in which God created everything that exists. The earth is only thousands of years old, as determined by the genealogies in the Bible.	The idea that God created various creatures to replace other creatures that died out over millions of years. Each of the days in Genesis represents a long period of time (day-age view) and the earth is billions of years old.	The idea that there was a long, long time between what happened in Genesis 1:1 and what happened in Genesis 1:2. During this time, the "fossil record" was supposed to have formed, and millions of years of earth history supposedly passed.	The idea that God used the process of evolution over millions of years (involving struggle and death) to bring about what we see today.	The view that there is no God and evolution of all life forms happened by purely naturalistic processes over billions of years.

Any theory that tries to combine the evolutionary time frame with creation presupposes that death entered the world before Adam sinned, which contradicts what God has said in His Word. The view that the earth (and its "fossil record") is hundreds of millions of years old damages the gospel message. God's completed creation was "very good" at the end of the sixth day (Genesis 1:31). Death entered this perfect paradise *after* Adam disobeyed God's command. It was the punishment for Adam's sin (Genesis 2:16–17; 3:19; Romans 5:12–19). Thorns appeared when God cursed the ground because of Adam's sin (Genesis 3:18).

The first animal death occurred when God killed at least one animal, shedding its blood, to make clothes for Adam and Eve (Genesis 3:21). If the earth's "fossil record" (filled with death, disease, and thorns) formed over millions of years before Adam appeared (and before he sinned), then death no longer would be the penalty for sin. Death, the "last enemy" (1 Corinthians 15:26), diseases (such as cancer), and thorns would instead be part of the original creation that God labeled "very good." No, it is clear that the "fossil record" formed sometime *after* Adam sinned—not many millions of years before. Most fossils were formed as a result of the worldwide Genesis Flood.

When viewed from a biblical perspective, the scientific evidence clearly supports a recent creation by God, and not naturalistic evolution and millions of years. The volume of evidence supporting the biblical creation account is substantial and cannot be adequately covered in this book. If you would like more information on this topic, please see the resource guide in the appendices. To help get you started, just a few examples of evidence supporting biblical creation are given below:

Evolutionary Myth: Life evolved from non-life when chemicals randomly combined together to produce amino acids and then proteins that produced living cells.

The Truth: The chemical requirements for DNA and proteins to line up just right to create life could not have happened through purely natural processes. The process of converting DNA information into proteins requires at least 75 different protein molecules. But each and every one of these 75 proteins must be synthesized in the first place by the process in which they themselves are involved. How could the process begin without the presence of all the necessary proteins? Could all 75 proteins have arisen by chance in just the right place at just the right time? Dr. Gary Parker says this is like the chicken and the egg problem. The obvious conclusion is that both the DNA and proteins must have been functional from the beginning, otherwise life could not exist. The best explanation for the existence of these proteins and DNA is that God created them.

Gary Parker, *Creation: Facts of Life* (Master Books, 2006), pp. 20–43.

Evolutionary Myth: Stanley Miller created life in a test tube, thus demonstrating that the early earth had the conditions necessary for life to begin.

The Truth: Although Miller was able to create amino acids from raw chemicals in his famous experiment, he did not create anything close to life or even the ingredients of life. There are four main problems with Miller's experiment. First, he left out oxygen because he knew that oxygen corrodes and destroys amino acids very quickly. However, rocks found in every layer of the earth indicate that oxygen has always been a part of the earth's atmosphere. Second, Miller included ammonia gas and methane gas. Ammonia gas would not have been present in any large quantities because it would have been dissolved in the oceans. And there is no indication in any of the rock layers that methane has ever been a part of the earth's atmosphere. Third, Miller used a spark of electricity to cause the amino acids to form, simulating lightning. However, this spark more quickly destroyed the amino acids than built them up, so to keep the amino acids from being destroyed, Miller used specially designed equipment to siphon off the amino acids before they could be destroyed. This is not what would have happened in nature. And finally, although Miller did produce amino acids, they were not the kinds of amino acids that are needed for life as we know it. Most of the acids were ones that actually break down proteins, not build them up.

Mike Riddle, "Can Natural Processes Explain the Origin of Life," in *The New Answers Book 2*, Ken Ham, ed. (Master Books, 2008). See also www.answersingenesis.org/go/origin.

Evolutionary Myth: Living creatures are just a collection of chemicals.

The Truth: It is true that cells are made of specific chemicals. However, a dead animal is made of the same chemicals as it was when it was living, but it cannot become alive again. What makes the chemicals into a living creature is the result of the organization of the substances, not just the substances themselves. Dr. Parker again uses an example. An airplane is made up of millions of non-flying parts; however, it can fly because of the design and organization of those parts. Similarly, plants and animals are alive because God created the chemicals in a specific way for them to be able to live. A collection of all the right parts is not life.

Evolutionary Myth: Chemical evidence points to an earth that is billions of years old.

The Truth: Much of the chemical evidence actually points to a young earth. For example, radioactive decay in the earth's crust produces helium atoms that rise to the surface and enter the atmosphere. Assuming that the rate of helium production has always been constant (an evolutionary assumption), the maximum age for the atmosphere could only be 2 million years.[1] This is much younger than the 4+ billion years claimed by evolutionists. And there are many ideas that could explain the presence of helium that would indicate a much younger age than 2 million years. Similarly, salt accumulates in the ocean over time. Evolutionists claim that life evolved in a salty ocean 3–4 billion years ago. If this were true and the salt has continued to accumulate over billions of years, the ocean would be too salty for anything to live in by now. Using the most conservative possible values (those that would give the oldest possible age for the oceans), scientists have calculated that the ocean must be less than 62 million years. That number is based on the assumption that nothing has affected the rate at which the salt is accumulating. However, the Genesis Flood would have drastically altered the amount of salt in the ocean, dissolving much sodium from land rocks.[2] Thus, the chemical evidence does not support an earth that is billions of years old.

[1] Don DeYoung, *Thousands…not billions* (Master Books, 2005).
[2] John D. Morris, *The Young Earth* (Master Books, 2007), pp. 83–87. See also www.answersingenesis.org/go/salty.

Despite the claims of many scientists, if you examine the evidence objectively, it is obvious that evolution and millions of years have not been proven. You can be confident that if you teach that what the Bible says is true, you won't go wrong. Instill in your student a confidence in the truth of the Bible in all areas. If scientific thought seems to contradict the Bible, realize that scientists often make mistakes, but God does not lie. At one time scientists believed that the earth was the center of the universe, that living things could spring from non-living things, and that blood-letting was good for the body. All of these were believed to be scientific facts but have since been disproved, but the Word of God remains true. If we use modern "science" to interpret the Bible, what will happen to our faith in God's Word when scientists change their theories yet again?

Integrating the Seven C's

Throughout the *God's Design® for Science* series you will see icons that represent the Seven C's of History. The Seven C's is a framework in which all of history, and the future to come, can be placed. As we go through our daily routines we may not understand how the details of life connect with the truth that we find in the Bible. This is also the case for students. When discussing the importance of the Bible you may find yourself telling students that the Bible is relevant in everyday activities. But how do we help the younger generation see that? The Seven C's are intended to help.

The Seven C's can be used to develop a biblical worldview in students, young or old. Much more than entertaining stories and religious teachings, the Bible has real connections to our everyday life. It may be hard, at first, to see how many connections there are, but with practice, the daily relevance of God's Word will come alive. Let's look at the Seven C's of History and how each can be connected to what the students are learning.

Creation

God perfectly created the heavens, the earth, and all that is in them in six normal-length days around 6,000 years ago.

This teaching is foundational to a biblical worldview and can be put into the context of any subject. In science, the amazing design that we see in nature—whether in the veins of a leaf or the complexity of your hand—is all the handiwork of God. Virtually all of the lessons in *God's Design for Science* can be related to God's creation of the heavens and earth.

Other contexts include:

Natural laws—any discussion of a law of nature naturally leads to God's creative power.

DNA and information—the information in every living thing was created by God's supreme intelligence.

Mathematics—the laws of mathematics reflect the order of the Creator.

Biological diversity—the distinct kinds of animals that we see were created during the Creation Week, not as products of evolution.

Art—the creativity of man is demonstrated through various art forms.

History—all time scales can be compared to the biblical time scale extending back about 6,000 years.

Ecology—God has called mankind to act as stewards over His creation.

Corruption

After God completed His perfect creation, Adam disobeyed God by eating the forbidden fruit. As a result, sin and death entered the world, and the world has been in decay since that time. This point is evident throughout the world that we live in. The struggle for survival in animals, the death of loved ones, and the violence all around us are all examples of the corrupting influence of sin.

Other contexts include:

Genetics—the mutations that lead to diseases, cancer, and variation within populations are the result of corruption.

Biological relationships—predators and parasites result from corruption.

History—wars and struggles between mankind, exemplified in the account of Cain and Abel, are a result of sin.

Catastrophe

God was grieved by the wickedness of mankind and judged this wickedness with a global Flood. The Flood covered the entire surface of the earth and killed all air-breathing creatures that were not aboard the Ark. The eight people and the animals aboard the Ark replenished the earth after God delivered them from the catastrophe.

The catastrophe described in the Bible would naturally leave behind much evidence. The studies of geology and of the biological diversity of animals on the planet are two of the most obvious applications of this event. Much of scientific understanding is based on how a scientist views the events of the Genesis Flood.

Other contexts include:

Biological diversity—all of the birds, mammals, and other air-breathing animals have populated the earth from the original kinds which left the Ark.

Geology—the layers of sedimentary rock seen in roadcuts, canyons, and other geologic features are testaments to the global Flood.

Geography—features like mountains, valleys, and plains were formed as the floodwaters receded.

Physics—rainbows are a perennial sign of God's faithfulness and His pledge to never flood the entire earth again.

Fossils—Most fossils are a result of the Flood rapidly burying plants and animals.

Plate tectonics—the rapid movement of the earth's plates likely accompanied the Flood.

Global warming/Ice Age—both of these items are likely a result of the activity of the Flood. The warming we are experiencing today has been present since the peak of the Ice Age (with variations over time).

Confusion

God commanded Noah and his descendants to spread across the earth. The refusal to obey this command and the building of the tower at Babel caused God to judge this sin. The common language of the people was confused and they spread across the globe as groups with a common language. All people are truly of "one blood" as descendants of Noah and, originally, Adam.

The confusion of the languages led people to scatter across the globe. As people settled in new areas, the traits they carried with them became concentrated in those populations. Traits like dark skin were beneficial in the tropics while other traits benefited populations in northern climates, and distinct people groups, not races, developed.

Other contexts include:

Genetics—the study of human DNA has shown that there is little difference in the genetic makeup of the so-called "races."

Languages—there are about seventy language groups from which all modern languages have developed.

Archaeology—the presence of common building structures, like pyramids, around the world confirms the biblical account.

Literature—recorded and oral records tell of similar events relating to the Flood and the dispersion at Babel.

Christ

God did not leave mankind without a way to be redeemed from its sinful state. The Law was given to Moses to show how far away man is from God's standard of perfection. Rather than the sacrifices, which only covered sins, people needed a Savior to take away their sin. This was accomplished when Jesus Christ came to earth to live a perfect life and, by that obedience, was able to be the sacrifice to satisfy God's wrath for all who believe.

The deity of Christ and the amazing plan that was set forth before the foundation of the earth is the core of Christian doctrine. The earthly life of Jesus was the fulfillment of many prophecies and confirms the truthfulness of the Bible. His miracles and presence in human form demonstrate that God is both intimately concerned with His creation and able to control it in an absolute way.

Other contexts include:

Psychology—popular secular psychology teaches of the inherent goodness of man, but Christ has lived the only perfect life. Mankind needs a Savior to redeem it from its unrighteousness.

Biology—Christ's virgin birth demonstrates God's sovereignty over nature.

Physics—turning the water into wine and the feeding of the five thousand demonstrate Christ's deity and His sovereignty over nature.

History—time is marked (in the western world) based on the birth of Christ despite current efforts to change the meaning.

Art—much art is based on the life of Christ and many of the masters are known for these depictions, whether on canvas or in music.

Cross

Because God is perfectly just and holy, He must punish sin. The sinless life of Jesus Christ was offered as a substitutionary sacrifice for all of those who will repent and put their faith in the Savior. After His death on the Cross, He defeated death by rising on the third day and is now seated at the right hand of God.

The events surrounding the crucifixion and resurrection have a most significant place in the life of Christians. Though there is no way to scientifically prove the resurrection, there is likewise no way to prove the stories of evolutionary history. These are matters of faith founded in the truth of God's Word and His character. The eyewitness testimony of over 500 people and the written Word of God provide the basis for our belief.

Other contexts include:

Biology—the biological details of the crucifixion can be studied alongside the anatomy of the human body.

History—the use of crucifixion as a method of punishment was short-lived in historical terms and not known at the time it was prophesied.

Art—the crucifixion and resurrection have inspired many wonderful works of art.

Consummation

God, in His great mercy, has promised that He will restore the earth to its original state—a world without death, suffering, war, and disease. The corruption introduced by Adam's sin will be removed. Those who have repented and put their trust in the completed work of Christ on the Cross will experience life in this new heaven and earth. We will be able to enjoy and worship God forever in a perfect place.

This future event is a little more difficult to connect with academic subjects. However, the hope of a life in God's presence and in the absence of sin can be inserted in discussions of human conflict, disease, suffering, and sin in general.

Other contexts include:

History—in discussions of war or human conflict the coming age offers hope.

Biology—the violent struggle for life seen in the predator-prey relationships will no longer taint the earth.

Medicine—while we struggle to find cures for diseases and alleviate the suffering of those enduring the effects of the Curse, we ultimately place our hope in the healing that will come in the eternal state.

The preceding examples are given to provide ideas for integrating the Seven C's of History into a broad range of curriculum activities. We would recommend that you give your students, and yourself, a better understanding of the Seven C's framework by using AiG's *Answers for Kids* curriculum. The first seven lessons of this curriculum cover the Seven C's and will establish a solid understanding of the true history, and future, of the universe. Full lesson plans, activities, and student resources are provided in the curriculum set.

We also offer bookmarks displaying the Seven C's and a wall chart. These can be used as visual cues for the students to help them recall the information and integrate new learning into its proper place in a biblical worldview.

Even if you use other curricula, you can still incorporate the Seven C's teaching into those. Using this approach will help students make firm connections between biblical events and every aspect of the world around them, and they will begin to develop a truly biblical worldview and not just add pieces of the Bible to what they learn in "the real world."

Unit 1

Introduction to Ecosystems

Lesson 1 What is an Ecosystem?

Biomes

Supply list

String Yardstick/meter stick Magnifying glass Copy of "My Backyard Habitat" worksheet

Supplies for Challenge: Copy of "World Map" World atlas

What did we learn?

- What is ecology? **The study of plants and animals and the environment in which they live.**
- What is the biosphere? **The part of the earth in which living things exist—includes the atmosphere, surface of the earth, underground, and the water.**
- Give an example of something that is biotic and something that is abiotic. **Examples of biotic: plants, animals, fungi, bacteria. Examples of abiotic: rocks, man-made objects, soil, weather.**
- What is flora? **Plants.**
- What is fauna? **Animals.**

Taking it further

- What factor has the greatest effect on the plants and animals that live in a particular ecosystem? **The climate.**
- How does your habitat change throughout the day? **Moving from the home to school or a store, going to the park or other area of activity.**
- List some ways that climate affects the habitats of people. **The houses they live in, the clothes they wear, the activities they participate in, and the foods that are readily available.**

Niches

What's your job?

Supply list

Jar Dark soil Sand Oats Earthworms Dark construction paper Tape
3-ring binder 9 dividers for the notebook

What did we learn?

- What is a niche? **The roles played by the plant or animal within its environment.**
- Name two factors that determine an animal's niche. **What it eats, what eats it, how it acts, things it can do, and its relationships with other animals.**
- What is a population? **The total number of a single species in a given area.**
- What is a community? **All of the populations in a given area.**
- What are two different kinds of niches an animal can have? **The niche a species has within the whole community and the niche a particular organism has within its species/colony.**

Taking it further

- What different niches do you fill in your family and in your community? **Child, sibling, cook, student, team member, performer, etc.**
- How does competition for food and other resources affect the niche of a plant or animal? **Competition occurs when there are limited resources. This limits the population of a species. It may result in certain plants or animals being aggressive or having specialized roles.**

Challenge: What's My Niche?

The following lists are not exhaustive; there are many other possible answers:

- Tree: **A tree serves many purposes. It is a home to many animals such as birds, squirrels, and insects. It provides shade and protection. The tree adds oxygen to the air and makes food for many animals when it performs photosynthesis. Some trees provide food through their leaves, fruit, and seeds. Trees hold the soil with their roots and draw water up from underground. They use some water for photosynthesis and release other water into the air.**
- Robin: **A robin eats insects and seeds and uses materials in its area to build its nest. Sometimes a robin becomes food for other animals such as cats or coyotes. Robins migrate so they provide these functions in different areas at different times. Robins sing which not only pleases people, but attracts a mate or drives away competitors. The robin's droppings help fertilize the ground helping new plants to grow.**
- Mouse: **A mouse eats plants and small insects. It builds its home in many different areas including underground, in hollows of a tree, in buildings, and more. Mice chew up nearly any available material to make their nests. Mice become food for many animals such as owls and snakes. Mice also become the home of fleas and other small insects. Mice can be carriers of diseases. Their droppings also help fertilize the ground.**
- Wolf: **A wolf moves over a large area of land so it affects many plants and animals. It is a predator that eats many smaller animals including rabbits, prairie dogs, fish, and even mice. Packs of wolves often attack larger animals such as deer and elk. It makes its home in burrows and may become a nuisance to farmers and ranchers.**

- Grass—**Grass is found in nearly every part of the world. It serves many roles. It performs photosynthesis so it removes carbon dioxide from the air and adds oxygen to the air. Its leaves, seeds, and roots provide food for many different animals from deer and elk to wildebeests and elephants. Grass can also be a decorative part of a person's yard.**

Food Chains

Does it have links?

Supply list

Drawing materials

What did we learn?

- What is a food chain? **A series of organisms in the order in which they feed on one another.**
- What is a producer? **A plant—something that makes its own food.**
- What is a consumer? **An organism that feeds on other organisms.**
- What is a food web? **Interconnecting food chains.**
- List two herbivores. **Deer, antelope, cattle, horses.**
- List two carnivores. **Wolf, coyote, weasel, lion, snake.**
- List two omnivores. **Bear, man, raccoon, mice.**

Taking it further

- Is a black bear a first or second order consumer? **It depends on what it is eating. If it is eating plants, it is a first order consumer. If it is eating fish, it is a second or maybe even third order consumer, depending on what the fish ate.**
- Is man an herbivore, carnivore, or omnivore? **Some people choose to live a vegetarian lifestyle, so they would be considered herbivores, but most people eat producers and consumers and would be considered omnivores.**
- Explain how a food chain shows energy flow. **A food chain starts with a plant, which converts sunlight into energy. That energy is passed on to the animal that eats the plant. Some of that energy is used up and some becomes part of the animal's body. That energy is then passed on to the next consumer.**

Scavengers & Decomposers

Breaking it down

Supply list

Food chain and food web pictures from lesson 3

Supplies for Challenge: Drawing materials

What did we learn?

- What type of organisms eat dead plants and animals? **Scavengers.**
- Name two different animals that eat dead plants or animals? **Vultures, flies, earthworms, coyotes, opossums, etc.**
- What types of organisms are at the end of every food chain? **Decomposers.**
- Name two common organisms responsible for decomposition. **Bacteria and fungi.**

Taking it further

- Why is decomposition so important? **It is the process that frees up the elements that were stored in the tissues of the dead plant or animal so they can be recycled.**
- What physical law makes decomposition necessary? **The law of conservation of matter/mass.**

Relationships among living things

Depending on each other

Supply list

Copy of "Symbiosis" worksheet   Optional: Rock with lichen   Magnifying glass
Supplies for Challenge: Research materials on liver flukes   Drawing materials

Symbiosis worksheet

- Illustrate which species benefits, which is unaffected, and which is harmed in each relationship by filling in the chart with the following types of symbiosis.

Species B

Species A

	+	0	-
+	**Mutualism**	**Commensalism**	**Parasitism**
0	**Commensalism**	**Neutralism**	**XXX**
-	**Parasitism**	**XXX**	**Competition**

What did we learn?

- What is symbiosis? **A close relationship between two different species.**
- What is mutualism? **A symbiotic relationship in which both species benefit from each other.**
- What happens to each species in a parasitic relationship? **The guest benefits and the host is harmed.**
- Which species benefits in commensalism? **The host species benefits.**
- What is competition among species? **When two species compete for limited resources.**
- What is the name of a relationship in which neither species benefits nor is harmed? **Neutralism.**

Taking it further

- Why is competition considered harmful for both species? **When their resources are limited some plants or animals will not get what they need and may die or fail to reproduce. This could affect both species that are competing for the resources.**
- Explain how competition could keep the species from becoming too populated. **When there are not enough resources for everyone to live, some plants or animals will die or fail to reproduce. This will prevent the population from becoming too large.**

Challenge: Liver Flukes

- **The sheep liver fluke enters a sheep when it eats grass containing fluke larvae. The larvae enter the sheep's liver and mature. Inside the liver the mature flukes lay eggs which then move into the sheep's digestive system and then into the feces and leave the sheep. The eggs enter water where they are eaten by certain snails. Inside the snail the fluke reproduces. These new larvae leave the snail and swim to grass. On the grass the larvae lose their tails and form cysts which climb up the grass and wait to be eaten by sheep. Other flukes have similar life cycles which require multiple hosts.**
- **There is a parasitic relationship between the fluke and the sheep and between the fluke and the snail. There is commensalism between the fluke and the grass.**

Oxygen & Water Cycles

What comes around goes around

Supply list

Potting soil   Glass jar with lid   Grass or other plant   Camera or drawing materials
Supplies for Challenge: Research materials on the nitrogen cycle

What did we learn?

- How do photosynthesis and respiration demonstrate the oxygen cycle? **During photosynthesis carbon dioxide and water, which contain oxygen atoms, are absorbed. Glucose and oxygen are produced. Animals eat the glucose and breathe in the oxygen. During respiration these molecules are broken down to release the energy and to produce water and carbon dioxide for plants to use again.**
- What are the major steps in the water cycle? **Evaporation, condensation, and precipitation.**

Taking it further

- Water exists in three forms: solid, liquid and gas. What phase is the water in before and after evaporation? **It changes from liquid into gas.**
- What phase is the water in before and after condensation? **It changes from gas to liquid.**
- What phase is the water in before and after precipitation? **If the temperature is not too cold it stays as a liquid. If the temperature is cold enough the water can change from liquid to solid and comes down as snow or sleet.**

QUIZ 1

Introduction to Ecosystems

Lessons 1–6

Match the term to its definition.

1. _**N**_ Decomposer
2. _**D**_ Biotic
3. _**B**_ Ecology
4. _**L**_ Omnivore
5. _**E**_ Abiotic
6. _**F**_ Ecosystem/biome
7. _**K**_ Carnivore
8. _**C**_ Biosphere
9. _**G**_ Flora
10. _**I**_ Niche
11. _**H**_ Fauna
12. _**A**_ Habitat
13. _**J**_ Herbivore
14. _**M**_ Scavenger
15. Draw a food chain with at least three levels. Label the role of each organism (producer, consumer, etc.) **Accept reasonable answers.**
16. Draw a food web with at least six organisms. **Accept reasonable answers.**

Describe each of the following relationships.

17. Mutualism: **Relationship in which both species benefit.**
18. Parasitism: **Relationship in which one species benefits and the other is harmed.**

Challenge Questions

Short answer:

19. Why do animals generally not migrate from one biogeographic realm to another? **Biogeographical realms are separated by large natural barriers such as oceans, high mountains, or large deserts.**
20. Describe the niche of a butterfly. **As a larva the butterfly eats plants, its droppings fertilize plants, it uses the plants for shelter and for a place to make its chrysalis. Adult butterflies drink nectar and pollinate different plants. Butterflies provide food for birds and other animals and provide beauty for people to enjoy.**
21. What is carrying capacity? **Carrying capacity is the maximum population an area can support.**
22. How does the number of first order consumers in a given area compare to the number of second order consumers? **There must be significantly more first order consumers than second order consumers. A good rule of thumb is 10 to 1.**
23. What law makes the oxygen, water, and nitrogen cycles necessary? **Law of conservation of mass/matter**

Unit 2

Grasslands & Forests

Biomes around the World

Where are they located?

Supply list

World atlas showing temperature and rainfall for the world as well as location of various ecosystems
Copies of the blank Average Rainfall, Average Temperature, and Biomes world maps
Supplies for Challenge: Research materials on ecological succession Poster board
Drawing materials

What did we learn?

- Where is the tropical zone located? **Between the Tropic of Cancer (23.5° north latitude) and the Tropic of Capricorn (23.5° south latitude), centered on the equator.**
- Where is the northern temperate zone located? **Between the Tropic of Cancer and the Arctic Circle (66.5° N).**
- Where is the southern temperate zone located? **Between the Tropic of Capricorn and the Antarctic Circle (66.5° S).**
- Where are the polar regions located? **North of the Arctic Circle and south of the Antarctic Circle.**

Taking it further

- Why are the polar regions generally colder than the tropical regions even though they receive many more hours of sunlight each day during the summer? **The sunlight reaches the earth at a sharper angle and much of it reflects away from the surface of the earth. Also, snow and ice tend to reflect much of the sunlight rather than absorbing it, thus keeping the temperature colder.**
- What correlations do you see between the temperature and rainfall maps that you made? **Answers will vary, but there is generally more rainfall in warmer areas, excepting deserts.**

Grasslands

Swaying in the breeze

Supply list

Grasses growing in a natural area Flowering plants field guide Newspaper Heavy books
Cardstock or heavy paper Page protectors Copy of "Grasslands" summary worksheet

Supplies for Challenge: Grass plants Scissors Ruler Copy of "Growing Grass" worksheet

What did we learn?

- Name three characteristics of a grassland biome. **10–30 inches of rain per year, distinct wet and dry seasons, warm summers and cold winters, and grass is the primary plant with few trees and shrubs.**
- What are four different types of grasslands? **Prairie, savannah, pampas, and steppe.**
- Where can each of these grasslands be found? **Prairie—North America,; Savannah—Africa; Pampas—South America; Steppe—Europe and Asia.**

Taking it further

- Why are there few trees in a grassland? **There is not enough rain to support trees. Also, periodic fires kill trees and shrubs.**
- How do many plants survive extended periods of drought in the grassland? **Many plants, such as grass, become dormant until there is enough water to resume growth. Other plants have very long roots to reach water deep underground.**
- How can grass survive when it is continually being cut down by grazing animals? **The growth center of grass is at the bottom of the plant, near ground level, so it can continue to grow after its top is cut off.**

Challenge: Growing Grass worksheet

- How did cutting the grass affect its ability to grow? **It didn't.**
- Did one plant grow more than the others? **Answers will vary.**
- How does this experiment demonstrate God's provision for grassland animals? **Grass provides food for grazing animals, and continues to provide more food even when eaten over and over again.**

Forests

Filled with trees

Supply list

Copy of "Where Would I Live?" worksheet

Supplies for Challenge: Drawing materials

Where Would I Live? worksheet

Emergent Layer	**Bald eagle, flies**
Canopy	**Spider monkey, opossum, fruit bat, tree frog, lemur, flies, woodpecker**
Understory	**Fruit bat, hummingbird, tree frog, flies, woodpecker**
Shrub Layer	**Monarch butterfly, hummingbird, flies**
Herb Layer	**Monarch butterfly, hummingbird, flies**
Floor	**Termites, black bear, rabbit, ibis, deer, flies**

What did we learn?

- What are the major plants in a forest? **Trees.**

- What are the six layers of a forest? **Emergent layer, canopy, understory, shrub, herb, and floor.**
- Which layer forms the roof of the forest? **Canopy.**
- Name three kinds of forests. **Deciduous, coniferous, tropical rainforest.**

Taking it further

- Why is the forest floor relatively dark? **The trees grow close enough together for their leaves to block out much of the light.**
- Why is it important to study each layer of a forest? **Different plants and animals can be found in each layer so you must study all the layers in order to understand the whole ecosystem.**
- How might new trees find room to grow in a mature forest? **Room is made when older trees die and fall down or when trees are damaged in a storm. Also, trees can be cut down by people.**

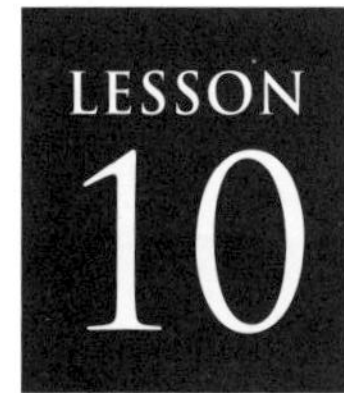

Temperate Forests

Can you see the forest for the trees?

Supply list

Copy of "Deciduous Forest" and "Coniferous Forest" summary worksheets
Copy of "Tree Identification" worksheet
Supplies for Challenge: Copy of "Forest Jeopardy" worksheet

What did we learn?

- What are some characteristics of a deciduous forest? **Dominant plants are deciduous trees, 30–60 inches of rainfall per year, 4 distinct seasons, warm wet summer and cold winter, trees lose leaves in the fall.**
- What are some characteristics of a coniferous forest? **Dominant plants are evergreen/coniferous trees, 12–33 inches of rainfall/precipitation per year, cold winters, many lakes.**
- What is another name for a coniferous forest in the far north? **Boreal forest or taiga.**
- What is a deciduous tree? **One that has broad flat leaves and sheds its leaves in the fall.**
- What is a coniferous tree? **One that has needle-like leaves that do not fall off and has cones instead of flowers.**

Taking it further

- What are some ways that plants in temperate forests were designed to withstand the cold winters? **Deciduous trees lose their leaves;, coniferous trees have needles that are not damaged by freezing temperatures. Trees have thick bark which helps protect them from cold wind and snow.**
- What are some ways that animals in temperate forests were designed to withstand the cold winters? **Many animals hibernate; others go into a deep sleep. Still others migrate to warmer areas during the winter and return in the summer months.**
- Would you expect plant material that falls to the floor of the coniferous forest to decay quickly or slowly? Why? **The floor of the coniferous forest is relatively dry and often cold. This is not an ideal environment for bacteria to grow so material decays relatively slowly in the coniferous forest.**

Challenge: Forest Jeopardy worksheet

Accept all reasonable questions.

1. Oak, maple, and beech. **What kind of trees might you find in a deciduous forest?**
2. Roof of the forest. **What is another name for the canopy of the forest?**
3. Lichen, moss, and fungi. **What plants might you find growing on the floor of a forest?**
4. Shrub layer. **What layer in the forest is below the understory?**
5. 30–60 inches per year. **How much rain does a deciduous forest receive each year?**
6. 12–33 inches per year. **How much rain/precipitation does a coniferous forest receive each year?**
7. Tropical and polar regions. **Between which two regions do you find temperate forests?**
8. Boreal forest and Taiga. **What other names refer to a coniferous forest?**
9. Dall and big horn sheep. **What are some animals that are likely to live in a coniferous forest?**
10. Many lakes. **What geologic features are found in coniferous forests as a result of the glacier movement during the Ice Age?**
11. Duck-billed platypus. **What is one animal that is found only in the forests of Australia?**
12. Tallest trees of the forest. **What would you see in the emergent layer of the forest?**

Tropical Rainforests

Growing where it's wet

Supply list

Copy of "Tropical Rainforest" summary worksheet   Research materials

What did we learn?

- List some ways in which a tropical rainforest is different from a temperate forest. **Rainforest receives more rain (over 80 inches per year). Rainforest is always warm to hot—no cold winters. Rainforests have more different kinds of animals, but relatively fewer mammals.**
- Where are the rainforests located? **Between the Tropic of Cancer and the Tropic of Capricorn; in the tropical region.**
- What is an arboreal animal? **One that lives primarily in trees.**
- What is an epiphyte? **A plant that grows on another plant without taking nutrients from it.**
- Name at least one epiphyte. **Orchid, fern, cactus, banyan tree.**

Taking it further

- Do you think that dead materials would decay slowly or quickly on the floor of the rainforest? Why? **Because the rainforest is warm and moist all the time, bacteria and other composters thrive, thus, dead material decays very quickly.**
- If you transplanted trees such as orange, cacao, or papaya trees, to a deciduous forest, would you expect them to survive? Why or why not? **Many tropical plants cannot survive the cold winters that are experienced in the deciduous forests. These plants would not be likely to survive.**

- Which animals are you most likely to see if you are taking a walk through the tropical rainforest? **Because many animals live primarily in the canopy, you would only see the ones that live near the floor or that visit the floor regularly. These might include lizards and snakes, capybaras, a few birds, and lots of insects. You would probably not see monkeys except from afar.**

QUIZ 2 Grasslands & Forests

Lessons 7–11

Mark each statement as either True or False.

1. **_T_** A puddle of water could be considered an ecosystem.
2. **_T_** The amount of sunlight hitting the earth is affected by the tilt of the earth.
3. **_F_** Polar regions are near the equator.
4. **_F_** It is uncommon to have a fire in a grassland.
5. **_T_** Grazing animals are specially designed to eat grass.
6. **_F_** Burrowing animals make it harder for grass to grow.
7. **_T_** Trees are the dominant plants in a forest.
8. **_F_** Temperate forests are located near the equator.
9. **_T_** Arboreal animals spend most of their time in trees.
10. **_F_** Epiphytes are animals that live on the forest floor.
11. **_T_** Rainforests receive over 80 inches of rain each year.
12. **_F_** Pampas grass is very short.
13. **_T_** Tropical rainforests are located near the equator.
14. **_T_** Arctic tundra is located in polar regions.
15. **_T_** Rainfall and sunlight help determine the ecosystem that will develop.

Short answer:

16. Give three different names for grassland. **Pampas, savannah, prairie, steppe**
17. List the six different layers of a forest. A. **Emergent layer** B. **Canopy** C. **Understory** D. **Shrub** E. **Herb** F. **Floor**
18. List two types of trees that you are likely to find in a deciduous forest. **Oak, elm, beech.**
19. List two type of trees that you are likely to find in a coniferous forest. **Pine, fir, spruce.**
20. Name three common products that originally came from the tropical rainforest. **Avocado, pineapple, papaya, cocoa, mango, cinnamon, cloves, allspice.**

Challenge Questions

Short answer:

21. Describe how succession might take place in a forest that was destroyed by a wildfire. **Small, quick-growing plants such as grass and dandelions will grow first. This will provide food for small animals such as rabbits and prairie dogs. These animals will attract predators such as coyotes and hawks. As the ground has more cover, there will be enough moisture for shrubs to begin to grow. The shrubs will provide habitat for nesting birds, squirrels and other animals. Tree seeds will germinate and begin to grow. Eventually, the trees**

will dominate the area again, reducing the sunlight to the floor and causing some of the smaller plants to die out. The trees will provide shelter and food for large animals such as deer and bears.

22. Explain how God designed grazing animals to survive in a grassland ecosystem. **Grazing animals have specially designed stomachs that allow them to digest grass. Different animals eat different parts of the grass plant, allowing the plant to feed more than one type of animal.**
23. Explain the purpose of each of the following parts of a tree.
    a. Outer bark: **Provides protection from hazards and harsh weather.**
    b. Phloem/inner bark: **Transports food from the leaves to rest of the plant.**
    c. Cambium: **Generates new phloem and xylem cells.**
    d. Xylem/sapwood: **Transports water and nutrients from the roots to the leaves.**
    e. Heartwood: **Provides strength and structure.**
24. Place the following ecosystems in order from least amount of rainfall to greatest amount of rainfall. **Grasslands, coniferous forest, deciduous forest, tropical rainforest.**
25. Explain the importance of the tropical rainforests on the medical field. **One-fourth of all medicines are derived from plants that come from the rainforest.**

UNIT 3

AQUATIC ECOSYSTEMS

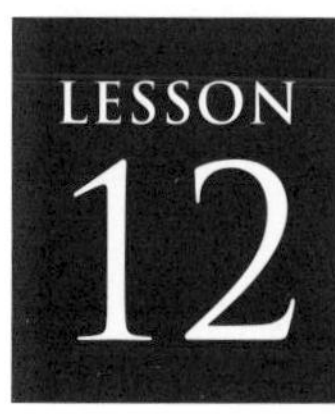

THE OCEAN

MARINE ECOSYSTEM

SUPPLY LIST

Copy of "Ocean" summary worksheet | Shallow pan | Water | Food coloring

Supplies for Challenge: Drawing materials

WHAT DID WE LEARN?

- How much of the earth is covered with water? **About 75%.**
- How much of the surface water of the world is in the ocean? **About 97%.**
- How many oceans are there? **Although there are 5 named oceans, they are all connected making only one ocean.**
- What are the three zones that the ocean can be divided into? **Sunlit (euphotic), twilight (disphotic), and midnight (aphotic) zones.**
- What are the three major groups of living organisms in the ocean? **Benthos, nekton, and plankton.**

TAKING IT FURTHER

- What might happen in the ocean if the currents stopped flowing? **The plankton would not be moved around and some areas of the ocean would have less food than now. This would cause some animals to die or leave the area. Nutrients in one area would be used up and plankton would die, causing other animals to die.**
- Why do most animals in the ocean live in the euphotic zone? **Photosynthesis can only take place where there is sufficient sunlight, so food is most abundant in the euphotic zone. Therefore, most animals will be found there.**
- Why might the aphotic zone occur at a shallower depth than 600 feet (200 m)in some areas? **The amount of sunlight that can penetrate the water depends on how clear the water is. If there is a significant amount of silt or other particles in the water, this will reduce the depth that the sunlight can penetrate.**

Coral Reefs

Underwater Wonderlands

Supply list

Copy of "Coral Reef" summary worksheet Modeling clay

What did we learn?

- Where will you find coral reefs? **In warm, clear water near the equator.**
- What is a coral reef made from? **Limestone from the exoskeletons of coral.**
- Where do corals get most of their energy? **From the algae that live with them.**
- What are the three main types of coral reefs? **Atoll, fringing, and barrier.**
- What are some of the animals that live in a coral reef besides corals? **Sponges, shrimp, sea stars, eels, turtles, octopus, fish, whales, etc.**

Taking it Further

- Why are coral reefs found in water that is usually less than 150 feet (45 m) deep? **The algae in the coral require sunlight for photosynthesis so coral cannot survive where there is not enough sunlight.**
- Why do corals grow best in swift water? **The moving water brings more nutrients which spurs growth.**

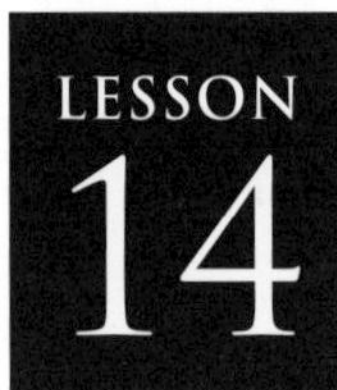

Beaches

Take a Walk on the Sand

Supply list

Copy of "Beach" summary worksheet Rocks Sea shells Plastic zipper bag Hammer
Safety goggles Towel Sand Magnifying glass

What did we learn?

- What is a beach? **The area where the water meets the land.**
- What are the two main kinds of beaches? **Rocky and sandy.**
- What is the name of the area of land that is covered at high tide and uncovered at low tide? **The intertidal zone.**
- What are some animals you are likely to see in a beach ecosystem? **Clams, mussels, crabs, oysters, starfish, barnacles, turtles, and gulls.**

Taking it further

- Why might you find different plants and animals on a rocky beach from those on a sandy beach? **A rocky beach provides more places for plants to anchor so a wider variety of plants and animals is likely to survive there.**
- How is new sand formed? **Waves erode rocks, shells, and coral to form new sand. Also, new sand can be formed when hot lava flows into cold water.**
- Explain how a beach can be in dynamic equilibrium. **Sand is made and deposited by the action of the waves while at the same time other sand and materials are dragged out to sea by the tide. If the amount deposited is about equal to the amount removed, the beach is said to be in dynamic equilibrium.**

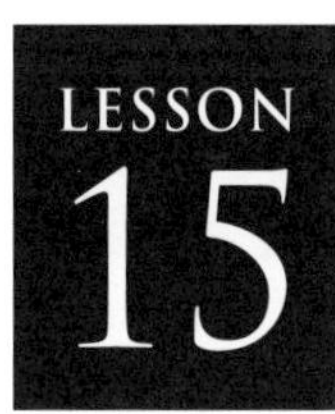

Estuaries

Where fresh and salty meet

Supply list

Copy of "Estuary" summary worksheet | 4 clear cups | Water | Salt | Eyedropper | Marker | Green and blue food coloring

What did we learn?

- What is an estuary? **An area where fresh water flows into saltwater.**
- Name three types of estuaries. **Salt marsh, salt meadow, and mangrove forest.**
- What are some plants you might find in an estuary? **Reeds, salt grass, mangrove trees.**
- Name several animals that you might find in an estuary. **Mud snails, marine worms, shellfish, mullet, flounder, sole, herons, terns, storks, pelicans, and sea lions.**

Taking it further

- Why is an estuary a very productive ecosystem? **The moving water stirs up nutrients that spur plant growth.**
- How do mangrove trees help coral reefs? **The trees help to filter out silt that might otherwise make the water cloudy.**
- Why is the salt level in the water constantly changing in an estuary? **Fresh water and saltwater do not easily mix. There is a constant flow of fresh water and a changing flow of saltwater due to tides so the salt level is changing. Seasonal changes in weather also affect salt levels.**
- Why might you find different animals in the same location at different times of the year? **Many animals migrate and spend different parts of the year in different locations.**

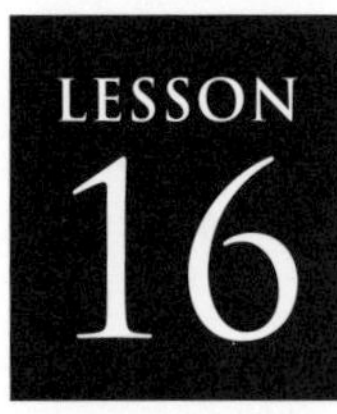

Lakes & Ponds

It's fresh

Supply list

Copy of "Lakes & Ponds" summary worksheet   2 clear cups   Water   Salt   Thermometer
Marker   Copy of "Watching Water Freeze" worksheet

Supplies for Challenge: Copy of "Great Lakes Fact Sheet"

What did we learn?

- What is a lake? **A large body of fresh water.**
- What is a pond? **A lake that is not deep enough to have a dark zone.**
- What are two ways that lakes were formed in the past? **Some lakes were dug out by glaciers; others have formed in craters of extinct volcanoes. It is likely that many of the lakes formed as a result of the Great Flood.**
- What is an overturn? **It is when colder water on the top of a lake rapidly sinks causing warmer water to rise.**
- What is an algae bloom? **A rapid growth in algae.**

Taking it further

- Why is overturn important to lake ecosystems? **It releases nutrients and oxygen that become trapped in the mud at the bottom of the lake.**
- Why does an algae bloom often occur in a lake in the spring? **Overturn occurs in the spring and releases nutrients that algae need to grow, causing algae to grow quickly.**
- In which lake zone would you expect to find most small creatures like rotifers? **They will most likely be in the sunlit zone because they eat algae, and algae need sunlight.**
- What would happen to fish during the winter if ice did not float? **As ice began to fill up the bottom of the lake, the fish would be forced to move up in the lake. Eventually the whole lake could freeze and the fish would die.**

Challenge: Great Lakes Fact Sheet

Answers may vary depending on the source. These numbers are from the EPA.

Feature	Lake Superior	Lake Michigan	Lake Huron	Lake Erie	Lake Ontario
Average Depth	**483 feet 147 meters**	**279 feet 85 meters**	**195 feet 59 meters**	**62 feet 19 meters**	**283 feet 86 meters**
Maximum Depth	**1322 feet 406 meters**	**925 feet 282 meters**	**750 feet 229 meters**	**210 feet 64 meters**	**802 feet 244 meters**
Volume	**2900 miles^3 12,100 km^3**	**1180 miles^3 4920 km^3**	**850 miles^3 3540 km^3**	**116 miles^3 484 km^3**	**393 miles^3 1640 km^3**
Major cities that border it	**Duluth, MN Sault Ste. Marie, ON Thunder Bay, ON Marquette, MI**	**Chicago, IL Gary, IN Green Bay, WI Milwaukee, WI**	**Sarnia, ON Port Huron, MI Bay City, MI**	**Buffalo, NY Cleveland, OH Erie, PA Toledo, OH**	**Hamilton, ON Kingston, ON Oshawa, ON Rochester, NY Toronto, ON Mississauga, ON**

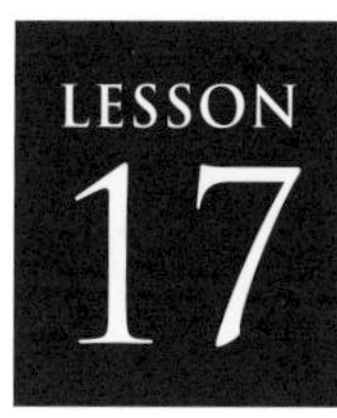

Rivers & Streams

Flowing water

Supply list

Copy of "Rivers & Streams" summary worksheet
Copy of "Rivers of the World" map
World atlas

Supplies for Challenge: Copy of "Rivers Fact Sheet"

What did we learn?

- What is a river? **A moving body of fresh water.**
- Where does most of the energy for a river ecosystem come from? **Plant material that falls into the river.**
- Name some plants you might find in a river ecosystem. **Grasses, pussy willows, alders, elkslip, and willow trees.**
- What is a tributary? **A smaller river or stream that flows into a larger river.**
- What is the riparian zone? **The area along the banks of a river.**

Taking it further

- Why do fewer plants grow in the water of a river than in a lake or ocean? **The current of the river makes it difficult for plants to stay in one place, and most plants need to stay anchored to survive.**
- Would you expect a river to be larger at a higher elevation or a lower elevation? **In general, because tributaries are adding water to a river as it flows downhill, you would expect the river to be smaller at higher elevations and larger at lower elevations.**
- Do rivers move faster over steep ground or in relatively flat areas? **Gravity is what causes water to flow, so water will flow faster over steeper ground.**
- Would you expect water to cause more erosion in a steep area or in a relatively flat area? **The faster water is moving, the more erosion it can cause, so more erosion will occur in steeper areas.**

Challenge: Rivers Fact Sheet

River	Length	Size of river basin	Discharge at mouth	Countries or states it flows through	Major tributaries
Amazon	**3920 mi 6308 km**	**2,270,000 sq. mi 7,050,000 sq. km**	**219,000 cu. meters/sec.**	**Peru, Brazil, Columbia, Venezuela, Bolivia**	**Negro, Tocantins**
Congo	**2900 mi 4700 km**	**1,440,000 sq. mi 3,822,000 sq. km**	**42,000 cu. meters/sec.**	**African Republic, Republic of the Congo, Angola, Zambia, Tanzania**	**Ubangi River, Aruwimi, Kasai, Lomami**
Nile	**4180 mi 6727 km**	**1,312,000 sq. mi 3,40,000 sq. km**	**2830 cu. meters/sec.**	**Ethiopia, Sudan, Egypt, Rwanda, Tanzania, Uganda, Burundi, Dem, Rep. of Congo, Eritrea, Kenya**	**White Nile, Blue Nile**

Mississippi	2320 mi 3734 km	1,151,000 sq. mi 2,981,000 sq. km	12,743 cu. meters/sec.	USA: MN, WI, IA, IL, MO, KY, TN, AR, LA, MS	Ohio, Missouri, Arkansas, Tennessee
Yangtze	3964 mi 6379 km	680,000 sq. mi 1,970,000 sq. km	35,000 cu. meters/sec.	China	Yalong, Minjiang, Jialing, Tuo he, Han
Rio De La Plata	2795 mi 4500 km	1,197,000 sq. mi 3,100,000 sq. km	17,100 cu. meters/sec.	Argentina, Uraguay	Paraguay, Pilcomayo, Parana, Uraguay
Hwang Ho/ Yellow	3395 mi 5464 km	290,000 sq. mi 745,000 sq. km	2,571 cu. meters/sec.	China	White, Black, Huang River
Orinoco	1300 mi 2100 km	340,000 sq. mi 880,000 sq. km	33,000 cu. meters/sec.	Venezuela, Brazil	Apure, Caura, Caroni
Yukon	2200 mi 3685 km	330,000 sq. mi 855,000 sq. km	6,430 cu. meters/sec.	United States (Alaska), Canada	Pelly, Porcupine Tanana
Volga	2290 mi 3688 km	533,000 sq. mi 1,380,000 sq. km	8,000 cu. meters/sec.	Russia	Kama, Oka, Moskva

Aquatic Ecosystems

Lessons 12–17

Write the correct term from the list below in each blank. Not all terms are used.

1. **_Phytoplankton_** is microscopic aquatic organisms that perform photosynthesis.
2. Plants and animals that live on the ocean floor are called **_benthos_**.
3. An **_atoll_** is a coral reef formed around a sunken volcano.
4. **_Nekton_** are animals that freely move throughout the ocean.
5. Where the ocean meets the land is called a **_beach_**.
6. An ecosystem where fresh water flows into the ocean is called an **_estuary_**.
7. Sudden rapid growth of algae is called an **_algae bloom_**.
8. Land along the banks of a river or stream is the **_riparian zone_**.
9. A **_tributary_** is a smaller stream or river that flows into a larger stream or river.
10. The **_inter-tidal zone_** is the part of the shore that is covered with water at high tide and uncovered at low tide.
11. A lake that is too shallow to have an aphotic zone is referred to as a **_pond_**.
12. A coral reef attached to land is a **_fringing reef_**.
13. **_Plankton_** are plants and animals that move with the ocean currents.
14. The layer of water that sunlight is able to penetrate is the **_sunlit/euphotic zone_**.
15. **_Overturn_** is the rapid exchange of cold and warm-water regions within a lake.

Short answer:

16. Briefly explain why you can expect to find more varieties of plants on a rocky beach than on a sandy beach. **Rocky beaches provide more cracks and soil for plants to anchor to.**
17. Why do coral grow only in relatively shallow water? **Coral rely on algae in their tissues to produce food for them. This requires sunlight for photosynthesis, so coral only grow where there is abundant sunlight.**
18. What is overturn in a lake? **Overturn is the rapid movement of cold water layers to the bottom of a lake and warm layers of water to the top of a lake.**
19. Why is an estuary a very productive ecosystem? **The water currents stir up and bring in a large amount of nutrients that spur plant growth.**
20. Which organisms form the base of the food chain in the ocean? **Plankton, particularly phytoplankton, produce most of the food that forms the base of the food chains in the ocean.**

CHALLENGE QUESTIONS

Mark each statement as either True or False.

21. _**T**_ Bioluminescent creatures produce light through a chemical reaction.
22. _**F**_ Coral bleaching occurs when there is too much bleach in the water.
23. _**F**_ Coral bleaching always causes the coral to die.
24. _**T**_ Algae and coral have a symbiotic relationship.
25. _**T**_ A dune system is an example of ecological succession.
26. _**F**_ A maritime forest usually has large trees.
27. _**T**_ The grass in a dune system helps to stabilize the dunes.
28. _**T**_ Dune grass must be tolerant to salt and wind.
29. _**F**_ Land can only be part of a single watershed.
30. _**T**_ The Mississippi River Basin is the largest watershed in the United States.
31. _**F**_ Water from the Mississippi River mixes quickly with the Gulf of Mexico.
32. _**T**_ The Great Lakes provide water and work for over 35 million people.
33. _**F**_ Invasive species are not a real threat to animals in the Great Lakes.
34. _**T**_ The Great Lakes can generate their own weather systems.
35. _**F**_ The Mississippi River has the largest volume of any river.
36. _**T**_ The Nile River is one of the longest rivers in the world.
37. _**T**_ River ecosystems vary as the speed of the river changes.
38. _**T**_ The Volga River is an important ecosystem in Russia.
39. _**T**_ The Amazon River has the largest watershed in the world.
40. _**F**_ Bioluminescent creatures live primarily in the sunlit zone.

Unit 4

Extreme Ecosystems

Lesson 18

Tundra

Is it frozen?

Supply list

Copy of "Tundra" summary worksheet   Small box   White cotton balls   Large bowl
White tissue paper or white quilt batting   Photos of Arctic animals with white fur or feathers
Two pairs of gloves (one pair must fit inside the other, for example one could be cotton gardening gloves and the other could be leather work gloves)   Ice

What did we learn?

- Where is most tundra located? **In the northern regions of Alaska, Canada, Greenland, Scandinavia, and Russia.**
- What is permafrost? **The layer below the surface that never thaws, even in summer.**
- What kind of plants grow in the tundra? **Small plants, including: flowers, small shrubs, rushes, sedges, heather, mosses, and lichens.**
- What are some animals you might find in the tundra? **Polar bears, Arctic foxes, caribou, moose, ptarmigan, Canada geese, Arctic hares, flies, and mosquitoes.**
- How much precipitation does the tundra receive? **6–10 inches a year.**

Taking it further

- Why do many animals in the tundra have white fur or feathers? **To provide them with camouflage from predators in the snow.**
- Why do many animals and plants have an accelerated life cycle in the tundra? **Because the growing season is only 50–60 days long.**
- Why do you think the temperatures are so cool in the summer when there is often 24 hours of sunshine? **Although the sun is up for many weeks, its light reaches the earth at a steep angle in the tundra so the energy is spread out. Also, the ice and snow reflect much of the light away from the ground, thus keeping it cool.**

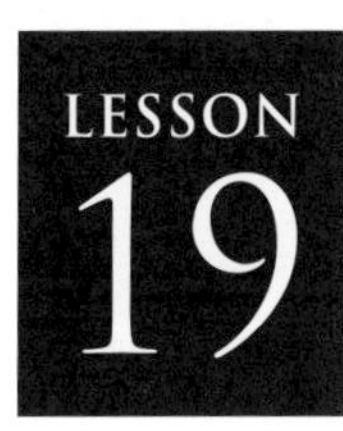

Desert

Sand and more sand

Supply list

Copy of "Desert" summary worksheet   Thin plastic bag (such as a produce bag)

What did we learn?

- What is a desert ecosystem? **One which receives less than 10 inches of rain per year.**
- How is a cold desert different from a hot desert? **Daytime temperatures drop below freezing in the winter in a cold desert but remain significantly above freezing during the day in a hot desert.**
- What are some plants you would expect to find in the desert? **Cactus, sagebrush, aloe, mesquite, Joshua tree, creosote bush, and desert trumpet.**
- What are some animals you would expect to find in the desert? **Mouse, toad, snake, lizard, badgers, ostriches, vultures, owls, and coyotes.**
- What is the difference between a Bactrian camel and a Dromedary camel? **Bactrian camels have two humps and longer hair; Dromedary camels have short hair and one hump.**

Taking it further

- In what ways are plants well suited for the desert environment? **Some can store large amounts of water; some have needles that do not lose water through transpiration; others have leaves with very few stomata; many have accelerated life cycles.**
- In what ways are animals well suited for the desert environment? **Most are nocturnal; some estivate; many have an accelerated life cycle.**
- Why does rain often cause flash flooding in the desert? **The ground is so dry and hard that water does not quickly soak in.**
- What are some dangers you may face in the desert? **Dehydration due to lack of water, heat stroke, freezing/exposure due to cold temperatures when the sun goes down, sand storms, and scorpion stings.**
- Why do salt flats often form in the desert? **Since water does not quickly soak into the ground, much of it evaporates, leaving dissolved salt behind. Over hundreds of years, this salt builds up to form salt flats.**
- Would you expect to find more salt flats in a cold desert or a hot desert? **More salt flats are found in cold deserts because cold deserts usually receive more water than hot deserts.**

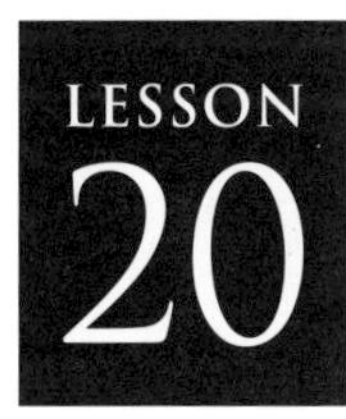

Oases

A refreshing spot

Supply list

Copy of "Oasis" summary worksheet   Several plant leaves   Plastic zipper bag

Supplies for Challenge: Research materials on desert products   Poster board   Drawing materials

What did we learn?

- What is an oasis? **An ecosystem in the desert where water is readily available.**
- What kinds of plants grow in an oasis? **Palm trees, shrubs, grass, and cacti.**
- What kinds of animals live in an oasis that don't usually live in a desert? **Fish, bats, warblers, and orioles.**

Taking it further

- Why is it often cooler in an oasis than in a desert? **The transpiration from the trees results in evaporation which cools the air. Also, the leaves of the trees block some of the sun.**
- Why are oases important for trade routes? **The only way to safely cross the desert in the past was by traveling from one oasis to another.**
- How might a man-made oasis change the ecosystem in a desert? **The water that is brought in will make it possible to grow plants that do not naturally grow there. This will provide habitat for animals that do no naturally live there. Also, it will add humidity to the air, thus cooling it down and possibly increasing the rainfall.**

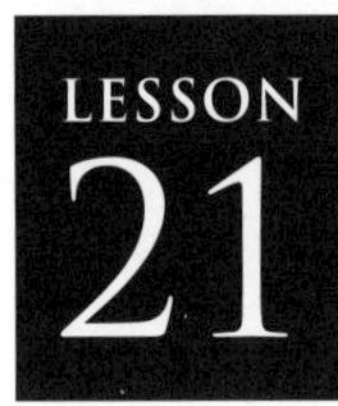

Mountains

Purple Mountain Majesties

Supply list

Copy of "Mountain" summary worksheet Art supplies Newspaper Paint Leaves Twigs Grass Small flowers Cotton balls

Supplies for Challenge: Research materials on the Himalayas

What did we learn?

- What ecosystems are you likely to encounter on mountains in temperate zones? **Grasslands, deciduous forests, evergreen forests, alpine meadows, and alpine tundra.**
- What ecosystems are you likely to encounter on mountains in tropical zones? **Rainforests, bamboo forests, heath, meadows, and tundra.**
- What is timberline? **The point above which no trees will grow.**
- What is snow line? **The point above which the snow does not completely melt, even in the summertime.**

Taking it further

- Why do the ecosystems change as you gain altitude on a mountain? **Temperature, rainfall, and oxygen levels change as you gain altitude, so different plants and animals will live at different altitudes.**
- Why don't you find every ecosystem on every mountain? **Different mountains are different heights. Most mountains are not high enough to experience all of the different ecosystems.**
- What other ecosystems are you likely to find on mountains that were not listed in the lesson? **Rivers, lakes, and ponds are abundant in most mountains.**
- How have glaciers influenced the shapes of mountains? **As glaciers receded at the end of the Great Ice Age, they dug out valleys, lakes, and other features in the mountains.**
- Why is there less oxygen as you gain altitude? **The gravitational pull of the earth becomes less as you go away from the center of the earth, so fewer air molecules are held close to the earth at higher altitudes.**

Chaparral

The Mediterranean climate

Supply list

Copy of "Chaparral" summary worksheet   Pictures of the chaparral

What did we learn?

- What is a chaparral ecosystem? **An ecosystem on hot, dry slopes in areas with mild, rainy winters.**
- What are two other names for chaparral? **Mediterranean ecosystem or maquis.**
- Name some plants you might find in the chaparral. **Scrub oak, live oak, yucca, buckbrush, and trefoil.**
- Name some animals you might find in the chaparral. **Woodrat, rabbit, fox, coyote, bobcat, quail, jay, wren, and sparrow.**
- What animal might you find in the Australian chaparral that you would not find in the American chaparral? **Koala.**

Taking it further

- What conditions make fire likely in the chaparral? **Hot, dry summers with low humidity, thick shrubbery, windy weather, and lightning.**
- How are plants in the chaparral specially designed for fire? **Seeds from many species only germinate after a fire.**
- Should people try to put out fires that naturally occur in the chaparral? **This is a difficult question to answer. Certainly if people's property is in danger the fires should be controlled. But studies have shown that fire is a natural part of the chaparral ecosystem and actually helps to keep it healthy, so many people think that natural fires should be allowed to burn when not endangering people or their property.**

Caves

Are they just holes in the ground?

Supply list

Copy of "Cave" summary worksheet   Houseplant   Box
Supplies for Challenge: Drawing materials

What did we learn?

- What is a cave? **A hole or cavern inside a mountain or underground.**
- What kinds of plants will you find in a cave ecosystem? **There are no plants inside the cave; a few may be growing near the entrance.**
- What are the three categories of animals in a cave ecosystem? **Trogloxenes, troglophiles, and troglobites.**

- Explain the different habits of each category of cave animal. **Trogloxenes visit the cave but do not spend their whole lives there. Troglophiles like to live in caves, but can live outside of a cave. Troglobites live their entire lives in a cave.**
- What is the main source of nutrients in a cave ecosystem? **Bat guano.**

Taking it further

- Why is a cave considered a low energy ecosystem? **There are no plants, so all energy must be brought in from the outside. This limits the amount of energy in the ecosystem.**
- Why can a rise in temperature inside a cave threaten the ecosystem? **Increased temperature means increased metabolism for cold-blooded animals, requiring more food, which may not be available.**
- What sense is least useful in a cave? **Sight.**
- What senses are most useful in a cave? **Hearing, smell, and touch are more useful than sight or taste.**

Extreme Ecosystems

Lessons 18–23

1. Place the animals below in the ecosystem(s) you are likely to find them.

Tundra	Desert	Oasis	Mountain	Cave
Arctic fox	**Toad**	**Toad**	**Arctic fox**	**Scorpions**
Reindeer	**Lizards**	**Lizards**	**Moose**	**Bats**
Moose	**Snakes**	**Snakes**	**Ground squirrel**	**Crickets**
Canada goose	**Scorpions**	**Scorpions**	**Snakes**	**Crayfish**
Ground squirrel	**Camels**	**Camels**	**Bats**	
		Bats	**Mountain lion**	
			Big horned sheep	

Choose the best answer for each statement or question.

2. _**B**_ The layer of permanently frozen ground in the tundra is:
3. _**A**_ Which do not help plants survive in the tundra?
4. _**A**_ On average, how much moisture does the tundra receive each year?
5. _**A**_ On average, how much moisture does a desert receive each year?
6. _**C**_ Which of the following helps animals survive in the desert?
7. _**D**_ Which are you not likely to find in an oasis?
8. _**B**_ You would expect the temperature in an oasis to be ______ than in the desert?
9. _**D**_ Which ecosystem would not likely be found on a mountain?
10. _**A**_ What is the point above which no trees will grow?
11. _**C**_ Which is likely to increase as you go up a mountain?
12. _**A**_ Which animal are you likely to find only in Australian chaparral?
13. _**C**_ Which condition does not contribute to fire in the chaparral?
14. _**D**_ Which animal is most important to cave ecosystems?

15. **_C_** Which animals do not live in or visit caves?

16. **_B_** Which sense is least useful inside a cave?

Challenge Questions

Short answer:

17. List three ways that polar bears are designed to live in the tundra. **Layer of blubber, two coats of hair, webbed feet, white color, good swimmers, sharp claws, papillae on pads of feet.**
18. The largest hot desert in the world is the **_Sahara Desert_**.
19. Where is this desert located? **In northern Africa.**
20. How has this desert changed since the time of the Genesis Flood? **It used to be much wetter and supported animals such as elephants.**
21. List three major products that come from deserts. **Oil/petroleum, gold, diamonds, uranium, nickel, aluminum, sodium nitrate, copper, solar energy.**
22. What is the tallest mountain in the Himalayas? **Mt. Everest.**
23. Name three animals found only in the Himalayas. **Snow leopard, clouded leopard, Bengal tiger, red panda.**
24. List three possible fire cues for seed germination. **Heat, smoke, charred wood, oxidation, acids.**
25. What method do insect-eating bats use to find their food? **Echolocation.**

UNIT 5

ANIMAL BEHAVIORS

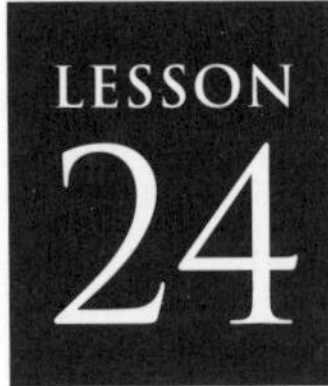

SEASONAL BEHAVIORS

IT HAPPENS EVERY YEAR

SUPPLY LIST

Research materials on monarch butterflies Paper Colored pencils

WHAT DID WE LEARN?

- What is hibernation? **A deep winter sleep in which the body's functions slow down greatly.**
- What is estivation? **A deep summer sleep similar to hibernation.**
- What is migration? **Moving from one location to another and then returning in order to survive the changing weather.**
- List three different kinds of animals that migrate. **Birds, whales, sea turtles, butterflies and other insects, caribou, salmon, etc.**
- What is the most likely trigger for seasonal behaviors? **The length of the day—changing number of hours of daylight.**

TAKING IT FURTHER

- How can animals know where they are supposed to go when they migrate if they have never been there before? **Some animals follow their parents, but many travel by instinct.**
- How do animals navigate while migrating? **Some use the stars, some follow scents, and others use landmarks.**
- Why might a group of animals move from one location to another, other than for their annual migration? **Changing climate conditions or natural disasters might make food scarce so animals will move to a new location. This is called immigration not migration because the animals do not usually return to the original location.**
- If you see a monarch butterfly in the fall and then see another one in the spring, how likely is it that you are seeing the same butterfly? **It depends where you live. If you live in Mexico, you might be seeing the butterfly when it arrives and when it leaves. But if you live in Canada, it is very unlikely that the same butterfly that flew south in the fall would ever live to make it back to the north.**

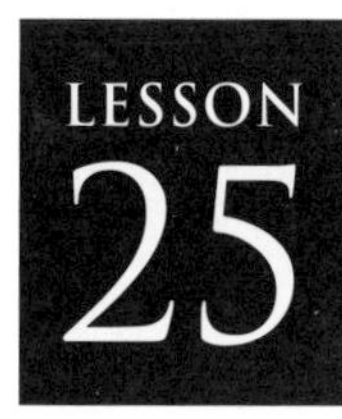

ANIMAL DEFENSES

A MATTER OF PROTECTION

SUPPLY LIST

Card stock or tagboard   Drawing materials   Pictures of animals

WHAT DID WE LEARN?

- What are three main ways that animals try to defend themselves? **Flight, trickery, and fight.**
- List three ways that animals can trick their enemies into leaving them alone. **Intimidation, ink, inflating their bodies, camouflage, etc.**
- How do some eels protect themselves? **They can shock their predators with an electric pulse.**

TAKING IT FURTHER

- Why do you think animals prefer to run away or frighten off enemies rather than fight? **Fighting is more dangerous. Getting away or making the enemy leave is more likely to keep the animal alive.**
- Why do many animals prefer trickery to running away? **Trickery uses up less energy than running away.**
- How might a defense also serve as an attack method? **An animal may use its teeth or claws to protect itself from its enemies and then use the same teeth and claws to attack its own prey.**

ADAPTATION

FITTING IN

SUPPLY LIST

Copy of "How was I Designed?" worksheet

HOW WAS I DESIGNED? WORKSHEET

Organism	Design features
Jack rabbit	**Has large ears for greater heat dissipation in hot environments.**
Woodpecker	**Has toes going both directions to grasp tree; has shock absorbing skull for drilling; has sticky tongue for getting insects inside a tree.**
Orchid	**Has roots that can absorb water from the air so they can grow on the sides of trees where there is adequate sunlight.**
Honey bee	**Has pollen baskets to collect pollen when getting nectar from flowers.**
Cactus	**Has needles to prevent loss of water; have the ability to store large amounts of water.**
Brown Bat	**Uses echolocation for flying and for catching insects; designed to hang upside down for long periods of time.**
Oak tree	**Loses its leaves in the winter.**

Prairie grass	**Has growing center near the ground so it can continue to grow even after being eaten over and over; goes dormant in winter.**
Barn owl	**Has great eyesight and hearing; has the ability to regurgitate indigestible materials.**
Chameleon	**Can change colors for camouflage and attracting mates.**

WHAT DID WE LEARN?

- What is an adaptation? **A physical characteristic or behavior that allows an animal to surive in its environment.**
- Are all helpful characteristics a result of a change in the organism? **No, many characteristics were part of the original created organism.**
- What process causes different species to develop among the same kind of animal or plant? **The selection of adaptations through natural selection.**

TAKING IT FURTHER

- How does natural selection work? **A kind of animal or plant can produce offspring with many different characteristics. If a particular characteristic makes an animal better suited for its environment, it will be more likely to survive and reproduce. Those offspring are more likely to have the trait that was beneficial, so they will be better suited to the environment.**
- Does natural selection require millions of years to develop distinct populations? **No, all of the animals began reproducing after the original pairs left the Ark only a few thousand years ago, and have developed into the many species we see today. There have even been observed cases of speciation.**
- Does natural selection require genetic mutation? **No. The information for great variety was available in the original created kinds. That variety can be selected for without mutations, though mutations provide more variety for selection to act on.**

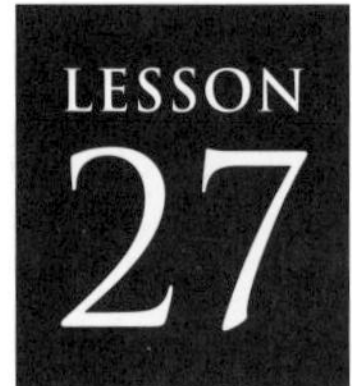

BALANCE OF NATURE

KEEPING IT WORKING

SUPPLY LIST (OPTIONAL ACTIVITY)

Cooking pot Grass Distilled water Jar Microscope Eyedropper
Microscope slides and cover slips Copy of "Growing an Ecosystem" worksheet
pH testing paper

WHAT DID WE LEARN?

- What is meant by the balance of nature? **A state in which the producers and consumers are in equilibrium.**
- Name two ways that the balance of nature is maintained in an ecosystem. **Predator/prey feedback and territoriality are the main ways. Flocking also affects the balance.**
- What are two ways that an animal might stake out its territory? **Singing, demonstrations, and scent markings.**
- What happens if a male cannot find a territory to defend? **He does not mate and waits until a territory opens up.**

Activity 25

Use the clues and the chart to determine the value of each letter, solve the cryptogram, and discover the classic joke.

$f > 3.5 + 5.5$

$f - 3 > e > i$

	n	e	i	f
5				
7				
9				
11				

n = ____
e = ____
i = ____
f = ____

$(c \div 4) + 11.5 = w$

$r \times c < l \times c$

	c	r	l	w
1				
2				
6				
12				

c = ____
r = ____
l = ____
w = ____

$o > (d + t) + 1$

$s > (d + t)$

$d < t$

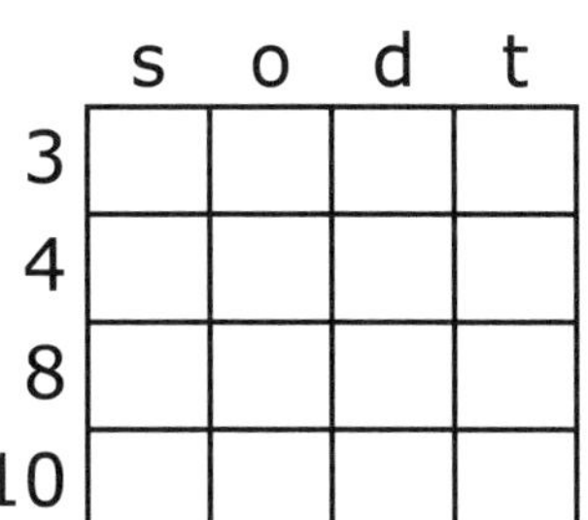

s = ____
o = ____
d = ____
t = ____

Cryptogram (Parentheses separate double digits; they have no other meaning.)

(12)hy (12)a8 4h7 2(10)mpu471 8(10) 2(10)63? 54
(11)(10)1g(10)4 4(10) 26(10)87 548 (12)593(10)(12)8!

_ hy _ a _ _ h _ _ _ mpu _ _ _ _ _ _ _ _ _?
_ _ _ _ _ g _ _ _ _ _ _ _ _ _ _ _ _ _
_ _ _ _ _ _ _ _ _!

Activity 26

Use the clues and the chart to determine the value of each letter, solve the cryptogram, and discover the classic joke.

$(w - s) + u = 10$

$u < 7$

	w	s	d	u
5				
2				
7				
9				

w = ____
s = ____
d = ____
u = ____

$m \times n = o \times 2$

$m \times a < n \times a$

	o	m	a	n
6				
4				
3				
10				

o = ____
m = ____
a = ____
n = ____

$c \times c \neq 64$

$e \times e \neq 144$

$i \times h = i$

$h \times e \neq 8$

	e	c	i	h
11				
8				
1				
12				

e = ____
c = ____
i = ____
h = ____

Cryptogram (Parentheses separate double digits; they have no other meaning.)

71(10)t 3(10)k(11)2 3528(12) 64 y65r 1(11)(10)9?
(10) 1(11)(10)9-b(10)49!

_ _ _ t _ _ k _ _ _ _ _ _ _ _ _ _ y _ _ r
_ _ _ _? _ _ _ _ _ - b _ _ _!

Activity 27

Use the clues and the chart to determine the value of each letter, solve the cryptogram, and discover the classic joke.

$a < e$

$e > i$

$u \geq 11$

$a > i$

	a	e	u	i
12				
10				
8				
3				

a = ____

e = ____

u = ____

i = ____

$o + w = p$

$o > 1$

$w > 5$

	o	c	w	p
11				
6				
5				
1				

o = ____

c = ____

w = ____

p = ____

$m \times s = 61 + k$

$m \div r < s \div r$

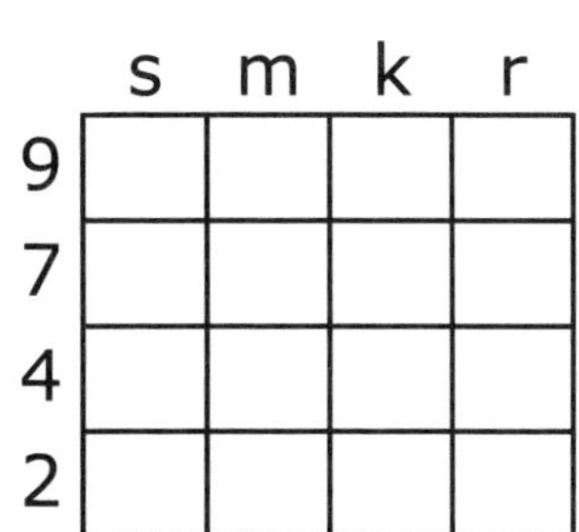

	s	m	k	r
9				
7				
4				
2				

s = ____

m = ____

k = ____

r = ____

Cryptogram (Parentheses separate double digits; they have no other meaning.)

6h8t 23nd 5f 7(12)931 d5 7(12)773(10)9 l32(10)? 648(11)!

_ h _ t _ _ nd _ f _ _ _ _ _ _ d _

_ _ _ _ _ _ _ l _ _ _? _ _ _ _!

Activity 28

Use the clues and the chart to determine the value of each letter, solve the cryptogram, and discover the classic joke.

10% of 200 = d + s
d > 9
b > s

	d	s	b	o
12				
9				
8				
3				

d = ____
s = ____
b = ____
o = ____

(h + u) × 100 = 800
i × r × r = 175
u < r

	i	r	h	u
7				
6				
5				
2				

i = ____
r = ____
h = ____
u = ____

g < c
g × c = 124 − 14
e > a

	e	a	g	c
11				
10				
4				
1				

e = ____
a = ____
g = ____
c = ____

Cryptogram (Parentheses separate double digits; they have no other meaning.)

W6y (12)7(12) t64 39t284 1n(10)l4 (10)3 t3
t64 941(11)6? 94(11)1284 7t w18 3v45 n7n4ty
(12)4(10)5448!

W _ y _ _ _ t _ _ _ _ t _ _ _ _ n _ l _ _ _
t _ t _ _ _ _ _ _ _ _? _ _ _ _ _ _ _ _ _ t
w _ _ _ v _ _ n _ n _ ty _ _ _ _ _ _ _ _!

Activity 29

Use the clues and the chart to determine the value of each letter, solve the cryptogram, and discover the classic joke.

$g \times s = (s + l + 5) \times s$

$s \times g = g$

	s	g	p	l
1				
3				
4				
9				

s = ____
g = ____
p = ____
l = ____

$e \times 10 > 100$

$r \times e > 60$

$r \times u < 13$

	c	u	e	r
2				
5				
6				
11				

c = ____
u = ____
e = ____
r = ____

$i \div k = 1.5$

$o \times 100 = a \times 70$

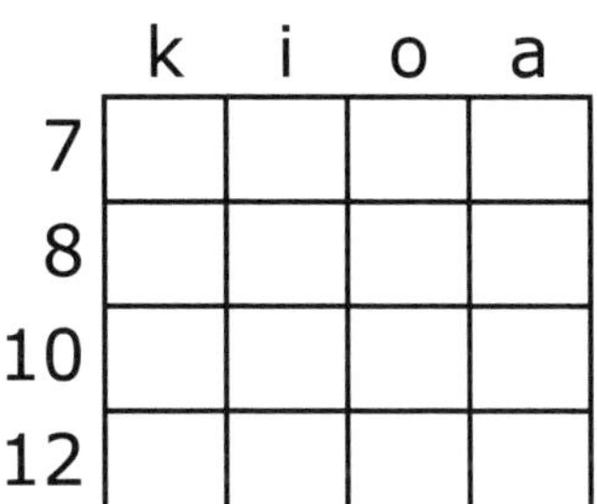

	k	i	o	a
7				
8				
10				
12				

k = ____
i = ____
o = ____
a = ____

Cryptogram (Parentheses separate double digits; they have no other meaning.)

Wh(10)t d7 y72 9(11)t wh(11)n y72 56711 47(12)17n 7(10)8 w(12)th (10) f726 3(11)(10)f 537v(11)6? (10) 6(10)1h 7f 977d 3258!

Wh _ t d _ y _ _ _ _ t wh _ n y _ _
_ _ _ _ _ _ _ _ _ _ _ n _ _ _ w _ th _
f _ _ _ _ _ _ f _ _ _ v _ _? _ _ _ _ h _ f
_ _ _ d _ _ _ _!

Activity 30

Use the clues and the chart to determine the value of each letter, solve the cryptogram, and discover the classic joke.

$(a \div w) + 2.25 = a$

$e \times a > n \times a$

	e	n	a	w
12				
4				
3				
2				

e = ____

n = ____

a = ____

w = ____

$(i - 2) \times g = 81$

$d \leq 7$

	t	g	d	i
11				
9				
8				
7				

t = ____

g = ____

d = ____

i = ____

$r \times 300 = p \times c \times o$

$c \div p = r + r$

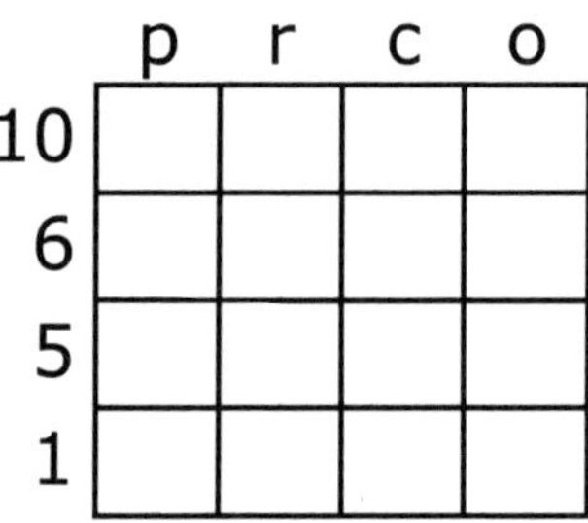

p = ____

r = ____

c = ____

o = ____

Cryptogram (Parentheses separate double digits; they have no other meaning.)

4hy 7(11)7 8h(12) 61329(12) 96 86 8h(12)
76(10)861? H(12) 43s 268 5(12)(12)l(11)29 4(12)ll!

_ hy _ _ _ _ h _ _ _ _ _ _ _ _ _ _ _ _ _

_ h _ _ _ _ _ _ _ _ _? H _ _ _ s _ _ _

_ _ _ l _ _ _ _ _ ll!

Detailed Solutions

Since there is only one answer to each problem, the order in which the clues are used does not affect the solution to the *Crypto Mind Bender®*. For example, if a problem has 5 clues, you might choose to apply clue 4 first and clue 2 second.

Page 1: Why don't you play cards in the jungle? There are too many cheetahs.

	a	w	s	n
1	+	—	—	—
2	—	—	+	—
3	—	—	—	+
4	—	+	—	—

Answers: a= 1; w = 4; s = 2; n = 3
Since *w* is greater than 3, *w* must be 4, the greatest number. Since *s* is greater than *a*, but less than *n*, *s* must be 2. Therefore, since *a* is less than *s*, *a* must be 1. *n* is then 3.

	i	r	h	t
5	—	+	—	—
6	—	—	—	+
7	—	—	+	—
8	+	—	—	—

Answers: i = 8; r = 5; h = 7; t = 6
If *h* plus 9 equals 16, *h* must be 7 for the equation to be true with the given numbers. Since *r* is less than 6, *r* must be 5, the smallest number. Since *t* is less than *i*, and only the numbers 6 and 8 remain, *t* must be 6, and *i* must be 8.

	e	j	o	c
9	+	—	—	—
10	—	—	—	+
11	—	—	+	—
12	—	+	—	—

Answers: e = 9; j = 12; o = 11; c = 10
If *o* plus 2 equals 13, *o* must be 11 for the equation to be true with the given numbers. Since *j* is greater than *o*, *j* must be 12, the largest number. Since *e* is less than *c*, *e* must be 9 and *c* must be 10.

Page 2: Why can't you tell a secret in a cornfield? Too many ears are listening!

	l	a	s	n
1	—	—	—	+
2	—	+	—	—
3	+	—	—	—
4	—	—	+	—

Answers: l = 3; a= 2; s = 4; n = 1
Since *l* and *s* are both greater than *a* and *n*, *l* and *s* must the largest numbers, either 3 or 4. Since *n* is less than *s*, *l*, and *a*, then *n* must be 1, the smallest number. Since *a* is larger than *n*, but less than *l* and *s*, *a* must be 2. If *l* minus *a* equals *n*, then *l* must be 3 for the equation to be true. *s* is then 4.

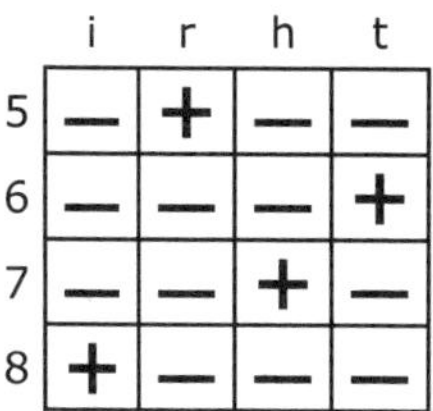

	i	r	h	t
5	—	+	—	—
6	—	—	—	+
7	—	—	+	—
8	+	—	—	—

Answers: i = 8; r = 5; h = 7; t = 6
If *h* plus *r* equals 12, then *h* and *r* must be either 5 or 7 for the equation to be true. Since *h* is greater than *r*, *h* must be 7 and *r* must be 5. Since *t* is less than *h*, *t* must be 6, the only number remaining which is less than 7. *i* is then 8.

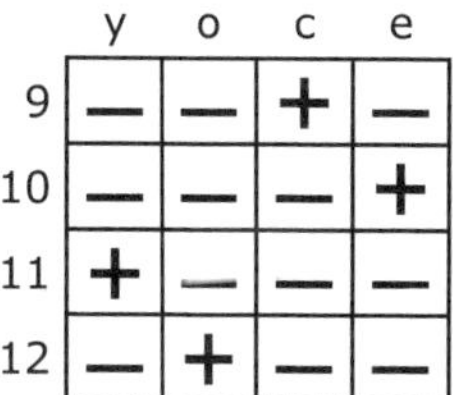

	y	o	c	e
9	—	—	+	—
10	—	—	—	+
11	+	—	—	—
12	—	+	—	—

Answers: y = 11; o = 12; c = 9; e = 10
If *o* plus 2 equals 14, *o* must be 12 for the equation to be true. Since *y* is greater than *c* and *e*, *y* must be 11, the largest remaining number. Since *c* is less than *e*, *c* must be 9 and *e* must be 10.

Page 3: What is a frog's favorite music?

Hip hop!

	f	n	s	i
1	+	—	—	—
2	—	—	—	+
5	—	—	+	—
6	—	+	—	—

Answers: f = 1; n = 6; s = 5; i = 2
If *n* minus *s* equals *f*, and *f* is less than 5, then *n* must be 6, *s* must be 5, and *f* must be 1 for the equation to be true. *i* is then 2.

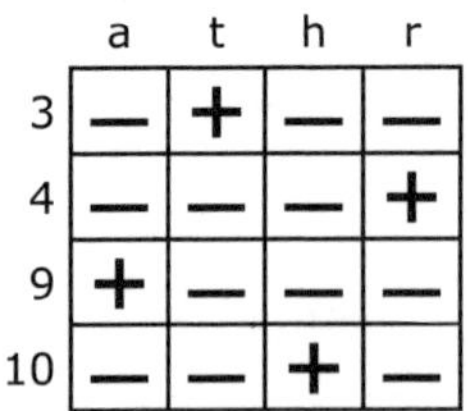

	a	t	h	r
3	—	+	—	—
4	—	—	—	+
9	+	—	—	—
10	—	—	+	—

Answers: a= 9; t = 3; h = 10; r = 4
If *a* plus *t* equals 12, then *a* and *t* must be either 3 or 9 for the equation to be true. If *a* plus *h* equals 19, *a* and *h* must be either 9 or 10 for the equation to be true; therefore, *a* must be 9, the only number used in both equations. Therefore, *t* must be 3, and *h* must be 10. *r* is then 4.

	p	e	c	m
7	—	—	+	—
8	—	—	—	+
11	+	—	—	—
12	—	+	—	—

Answers: p = 11; e = 12; c = 7; m = 8
If *p* equals *c* plus 4, and *m* equals *c* plus 1, *p* must be 11, *c* must be 7, and *m* must be 8 for the equations to be true. *e* is then 12.

Page 4: What do you call a fake noodle? An impasta!

	o	c	i	s
1	—	—	—	+
2	—	+	—	—
10	—	—	+	—
12	+	—	—	—

Answers: o = 12; c = 2; i = 10; s =1
If *i* equals *c* times 5, *i* must be 10 and *c* must be 2 for the equation to be true with the given numbers. Since *o* is greater than *s*, *o* must be 12, and *s* must be 1.

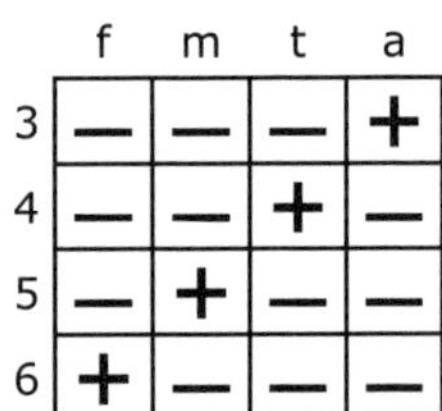

	f	m	t	a
3	—	—	—	+
4	—	—	+	—
5	—	+	—	—
6	+	—	—	—

Answers: f = 6; m = 5; t = 4;a= 3
Since *a* is less than both *m* and *f*, *a* must be one of the smallest numbers, either 3 or 4, and since *a* is not 4, *a* must be 3. If *m* is not 4 or 6, then *m* must be 5, the only number left. Since *f* is greater than *m*, *f* must be 6. *t* is then 4.

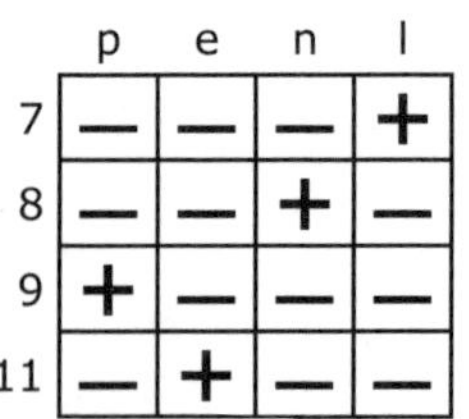

	p	e	n	l
7	—	—	—	+
8	—	—	+	—
9	+	—	—	—
11	—	+	—	—

Answers: p = 9; e = 11; n = 8; l = 7
If *e* is greater than 10, *e* must be 11, the largest number. If *p* is greater than 8, *p* must be 9. Since *n* is greater than *l*, *n* must be 8 and *l* must be 7.

Page 5: What did the traffic light say to the car? Don't look, I'm changing!

	g	i	c	a
1	—	+	—	—
2	—	—	+	—
8	+	—	—	—
10	—	—	—	+

Answers: g = 8; i = 1; c = 2; a= 10
Since *g* is greater than 7, *g* must be either 8 or 10. Since *g* is less than *a* minus *i*, *g* must be 8, *a* must be 10 and *i* must be 1 for the statement to be true. *c* is then 2.

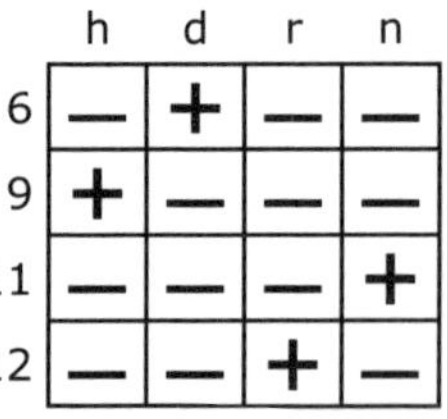

	h	d	r	n
6	—	+	—	—
9	+	—	—	—
11	—	—	—	+
12	—	—	+	—

Answers: h = 9; d = 6; r = 12; n = 11
Since *d* is less than both *h* and *r*, and is not 9, then *d* must be 6, the lowest number. Since *r* is greater than *h* and *d*, and is not 11, then *r* must be 12, the largest number. Since *h* is less than *r*, but greater than *d*, *h* must be either 9 or 11, and since *n* is not 9, it must be 11; therefore, *h* must be 9.

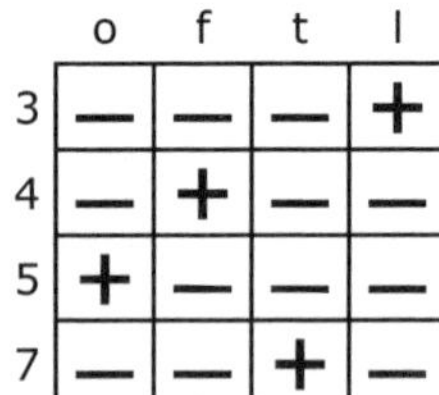

	o	f	t	l
3	—	—	—	+
4	—	+	—	—
5	+	—	—	—
7	—	—	+	—

Answers: o = 5; f = 4; t = 7; l = 3
Since *o* is greater than *f* and *l*, *o* must be either 5 or 7. Since *f* is greater than *l*, but less than *o*, *f* must be a middle number, either 4 or 5, and *l* must be a lower number, either 3 or 4. If *o* does not equal *f* plus *l*, then *o* does not equal 7, 8, or 9, the possible sums of *f* plus *l*; therefore, *o* must be 5. Therefore, *f* must be 4, and *l* must be 3, the only numbers lower than 5. *t* is then 7.

Page 6: Why did the boy eat his homework? Because his teacher said it was a piece of cake.

	b	a	r	h
4	—	+	—	—
6	+	—	—	—
8	—	—	—	+
10	—	—	+	—

Answers: b = 6; a= 4; r = 10; h = 8
If *b* equals *a* plus 2, *a* must be either 4, 6, or 8, and *b* must be either 6, 8, or 10, for the equation to be true. Since *r* is greater than 9, *r* must be 10. Therefore, *b* must be either 6 or 8, and since *b* is less than 7, *b* must be 6. Therefore, *a* must be 4 for the equation to be true. *h* is then 8.

	k	o	w	d
2	—	—	—	+
3	—	+	—	—
5	—	—	+	—
7	+	—	—	—

Answers: k = 7; o = 3; w = 5; d = 2
If *k* times 4 equals 28, *k* must be 7 for the equation to be true. If *o* plus *d* equals *w*, then *o* and *d* must be either 2 or 3, and *w* must be 5 for the equation to be true. Since *o* is greater than *d*, *o* must be 3, and *d* must be 2.

	s	i	c	e
1	+	—	—	—
9	—	—	+	—
11	—	+	—	—
12	—	—	—	+

Answers: s = 1; i = 11; c = 9; e = 12
If *s* times *c* equals *c*, *s* must be 1 since any number times 1 equals that same number. If *s* plus *i* equals *e*, *i* must be 11 and *e* must be 12 for the equation to be true. *c* is then 9.

Page 7: Why do gorillas have such big nostrils? Have you seen their fingers?

	g	o	n	k
12	—	—	+	—
11	+	—	—	—
10	—	—	—	+
9	—	+	—	—

Answers: g = 11; o = 9; n = 12; k = 10
Since *n* is greater than 11, *n* must be 12, the largest number. If *n* plus *o* equals *g* plus *k*, *o* must be 9, and *g* and *k* must be either 10 or 11 for the equation to be true. Since *g* is greater than *k*, *g* must be 11, and *k* must be 10.

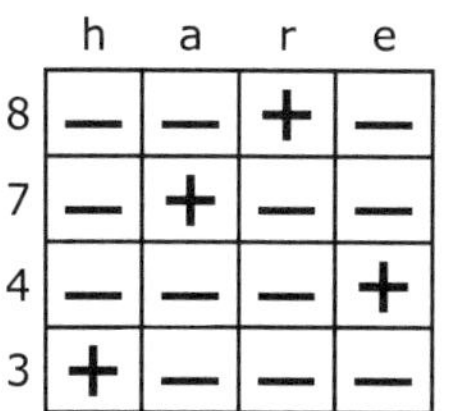

	h	a	r	e
8	—	—	+	—
7	—	+	—	—
4	—	—	—	+
3	+	—	—	—

Answers: h = 3; a= 7; r = 8; e = 4
If *h* times *h* equals 9, *h* must be 3 for the equation to be true. If *h* plus *r* equals *a* plus *e*, *r* must be 8, and *a* and *e* must be 4 or 7 for the equation to be true. Since *e* is less than *a*, *e* must be 4 and *a* must be 7.

	f	b	s	i
6	—	—	—	+
5	+	—	—	—
2	—	—	+	—
1	—	+	—	—

Answers: f = 5; b = 1; s = 2; i = 6
If *f* plus *i* equals 11, *f* and *i* must be either 5 or 6 for the equation to be true. If *s* plus *i* equals *f* plus 3, *i* must be 6, *s* must be 2, and *f* must be 5 for the equation to be true. *b* is then 1.

Page 8: How does a penguin build his house? Igloos it together!

	i	e	n	h
8	—	+	—	—
9	—	—	+	—
10	+	—	—	—
12	—	—	—	+

Answers: i = 10; e = 8; n = 9; h = 12
If *h* plus *e* plus *i* equals 30, then *h*, *e*, and *i* must be some combination of 8, 10, and 12 for the equation to be true. Since *h* is greater than *i* and *e*, *h* must be 12. Since *i* is less than *h*, but greater than *e*, *i* must be 10, and *e* must 8. *n* is then 9.

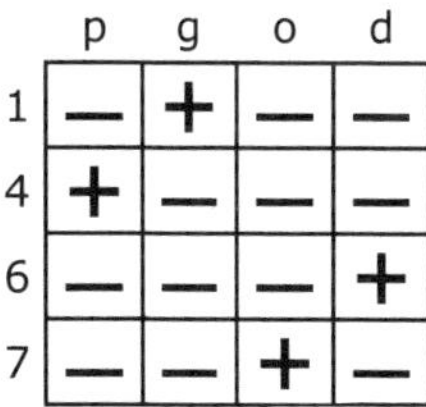

	p	g	o	d
1	—	+	—	—
4	+	—	—	—
6	—	—	—	+
7	—	—	+	—

Answers: p = 4; g = 1; o = 7; d = 6
If *p* times *g* equals *d* minus 2, *p* and *g* must be either 1 or 4, and *d* must be 6, for the equation to be true. If *p* is greater than *d* minus 5, *p* is greater than 1; therefore, *p* must be 4. Therefore, *g* must be 1. *o* is then 7.

	a	l	s	t
2	+	—	—	—
3	—	—	—	+
5	—	+	—	—
11	—	—	+	—

Answers: a= 2; l = 5; s = 11; t= 3
Since *s* is greater than *a*, *t*, and *l*, *s* must be 11. Since *a* is less than *t*, *l*, and *s*, *a* must be 2, the lowest number. Since *t* is less than *l*, *t* must be 3. *l* is then 5.

Page 9: What did one plate say to the other? Lunch is on me!

	n	l	d	m
1	+	—	—	—
4	—	—	+	—
8	—	—	—	+
10	—	+	—	—

Answers: n = 1; l = 10; d = 4; m = 8
If *l* times *m* equals 80, *l* and *m* must be either 8 or 10 for the equation to be true with the given numbers. If *l* times *n* equals 10, *l* and *n* must be either 1 or 10 for the equation to be true. Therefore, *l* must be 10, the only number used in both equations. *m* must be 8, and *n* must be 1. *d* is then 4.

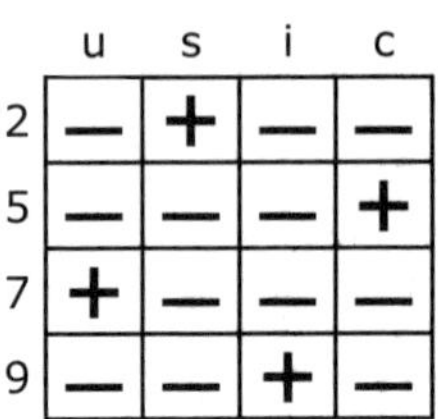

	u	s	i	c
2	—	+	—	—
5	—	—	—	+
7	+	—	—	—
9	—	—	+	—

Answers: u = 7; s = 2; i = 9; c = 5
If *u* times *c* equals 35, *u* and *c* must be either 5 or 7 for the equation to be true. If *u* times *s* equals *i* plus *c*, *u* must be 7, *s* must be 2, *c* must be 5, and *i* must be 9 for the equation to be true.

	p	e	h	a
3	—	—	+	—
6	—	+	—	—
11	+	—	—	—
12	—	—	—	+

Answers: p = 11; e = 6; h = 3; a= 12
If *p* times *a* equals 132, *p* and *a* must be 11 or 12 for the equation to be true. If *p* minus *e* equals 5, *p* must be 11 and *e* must be 6 for the equation to be true. Therefore, *a* must be 12. *h* is then 3.

Page 10: What did the pen ask the pencil? So what's your point!

	c	e	p	i
11	—	—	+	—
9	+	—	—	—
5	—	—	—	+
2	—	+	—	—

Answers: c = 9; e = 2; p = 11; i = 5
If *i* minus 2 equals *c* divided by 3, *i* must be 5 and *c* must be 9 for the equation to be true. Since *p* is greater than *c*, *p* must be 11, the largest number. *e* is then 2.

	w	a	d	n
12	+	—	—	—
6	—	—	+	—
4	—	—	—	+
1	—	+	—	—

Answers: w = 12; a= 1; d = 6; n = 4
If *w* divided by 3 equals *n*, *w* must be 12 and *n* must be 4, for the equation to be true. If *a* plus 5 equals *d*, *a* must be 1 and *d* must be 6 for the equation to be true.

	t	l	o	s
10	—	—	+	—
8	+	—	—	—
7	—	—	—	+
3	—	+	—	—

Answers: t = 8; l = 3; o = 10; s = 7
If *s* times 2 equals *t* plus 6, *s* must be either 7 or 8, and *t* must be either 8 or 10, for the equation to be true. Since *t* is less than 9, *t* must be 8. Therefore, *s* must be 7. Since *o* is greater than *s*, *o* must be 10, the largest remaining number. *l* is then 3.

Page 11: What is the most expensive fish? A goldfish!

	a	w	s	n
12	—	+	—	—
7	+	—	—	—
9	—	—	+	—
6	—	—	—	+

Answers: a = 7; w = 12; s= 9; n = 6
Since both *w* and *s* are greater than *a* and *n*, *w* and *s* must be either 9 or 12, the largest numbers. Since *n* is less than *s*, *w*, and *a*, *n* must be 6, the smallest number. Since *a* is greater than *n*, but less than *w* and *s*, *a* must be 7. If *w* plus 4 equals *s* plus *a*, *w* must be 12 and *s* must be 9 for the equation to be true.

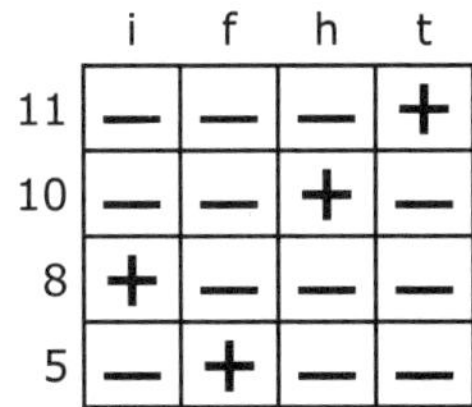

	i	f	h	t
11	—	—	—	+
10	—	—	+	—
8	+	—	—	—
5	—	+	—	—

Answers: i = 8; f = 5; h = 10; t = 11
If *h* divided by *f* equals 2, *h* must be 10 and *f* must be 5 for the equation to be true. Since *t* is greater than *h*, *t* must be 11, the only number larger than 10. *i* is then 8.

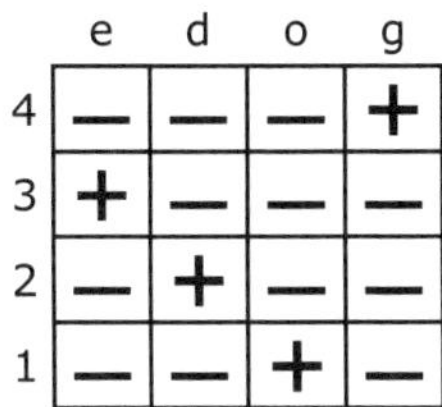

	e	d	o	g
4	—	—	—	+
3	+	—	—	—
2	—	+	—	—
1	—	—	+	—

Answers: e = 3; d = 2; o = 1; g = 4
If *o* plus *d* equals *e*, *e* must be either 3 or 4 for the equation to be true. Since *e* is less than *g*, *e* must be 3, and *g* must be 4. If *o* times *d* equals *d*, *o* must be 1, and *d* must be 2, since any number times 1 equals the number by which it was multiplied.

Page 12: Why did the math book cry? It had too many problems.

	h	e	o	b
11	—	—	+	—
8	+	—	—	—
5	—	—	—	+
2	—	+	—	—

Answers: h = 8; e = 2; o = 11; b = 5
Since *b* is less than 6, *b* must be 2 or 5, and since *e* is less than 3, *e* must be 2; therefore, *b* must be 5. Since *h* is less than or equal to 9, *h* must be 8, the only number remaining less than 9. *o* is then 11.

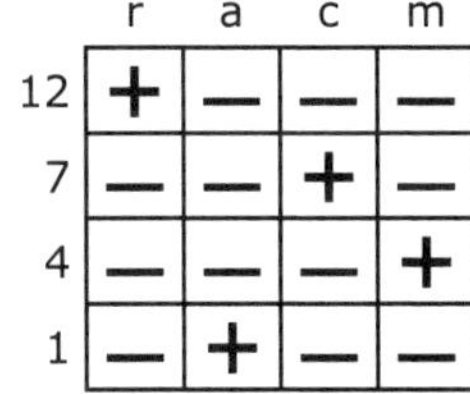

	r	a	c	m
12	+	—	—	—
7	—	—	+	—
4	—	—	—	+
1	—	+	—	—

Answers: r = 12; a = 1; c = 7; m = 4
If *r* divided by *m* equals 3, *r* must be 12 and *m* must be 4 for the equation to be true. If *m* plus 4 equals *c* plus 1, *c* must be 7 for the equation to be true. *a* is then 1.

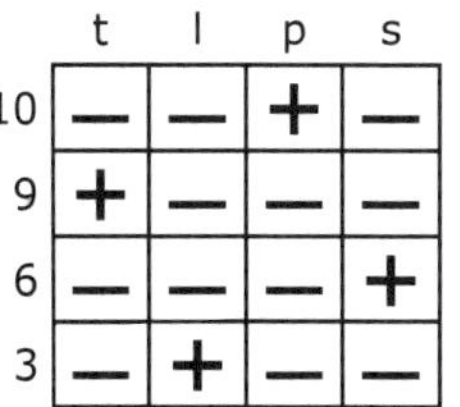

	t	l	p	s
10	—	—	+	—
9	+	—	—	—
6	—	—	—	+
3	—	+	—	—

Answers: t = 9; l = 3; p = 10; s = 6
If *s* times 2 equals *l* times 4, *s* must be 6 and *l* must be 3 for the equation to be true. Since *p* is greater than *t*, *p* must be 10, the largest number, and *t* must be 9.

Page 13: What do you call a bear with no teeth? A gummy bear!

	g	r	l	u
10	—	+	—	—
9	+	—	—	—
5	—	—	+	—
4	—	—	—	+

Answers: g = 9; r = 10; l = 5; u = 4
Since *u* is less than 5, *u* must be 4, the smallest number. If *l* is less than *u* plus 2, *l* must be 5, the only remaining number less than 6. Since *r* minus *g* equals *l* minus *u*, *r* must be 10 and *g* must be 9 for the equation to be true.

	e	t	y	o
11	—	—	+	—
8	+	—	—	—
3	—	+	—	—
1	—	—	—	+

Answers: e = 8; t = 3; y = 11; o = 1
If *e* equals 4 times 2, *e* must be 8. If *y* is greater than 10, *y* must be 11, the largest number. Since *o* does not equal *y* minus *e*, *o* is not 3; therefore, *o* must be 1. *t* is then 3.

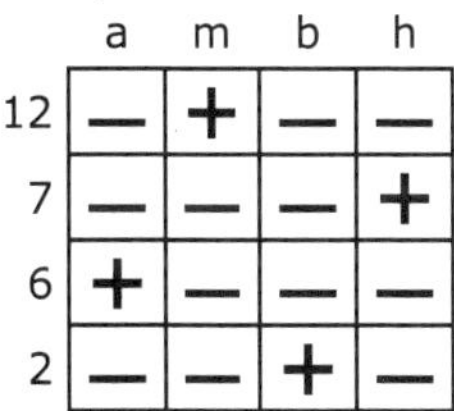

	a	m	b	h
12	—	+	—	—
7	—	—	—	+
6	+	—	—	—
2	—	—	+	—

Answers: a = 6; m = 12; b = 2; h = 7
If *b* is less than 4, *b* must be 2, the smallest number. Since *h* does not equal *b* plus *b* plus *b*, *h* is not 6. Since *h* does not equal *b* plus 10, *h* is not 12. Therefore, *h* must be 7, the only remaining number. Since *m* does not equal *b* plus *b* plus *b*, *m* is not 6; therefore, *m* must be 12. *a* is then 6.

Page 14: Why did the baseball player take his bat to the library? His teacher told him to hit the books.

	m	e	b	i
12	—	—	+	—
11	+	—	—	—
9	—	+	—	—
8	—	—	—	+

Answers: m = 11; e = 9; b = 12; i = 8
If *b* is not 9 or 11, *b* must be 8 or 12. If *e* is not 8 or 11, *e* must be 9 or 12. Since *b* minus *e* equals *m* minus *i*, *b* must be 12, *e* must be 9, *m* must be 11 and *i* must be 8 for the equation to be true.

	s	t	a	h
10	+	—	—	—
7	—	+	—	—
5	—	—	+	—
3	—	—	—	+

Answers: s = 10; t = 7; a = 5; h = 3
If *s* times *t* equals 65 plus *a*, *s* and *t* must be either 7 or 10, and *a* must be 5, for the equation to be true with the given numbers. If *t* plus *a* equals 12, *t* must be 7. Therefore, *s* must be 10. *h* is then 3.

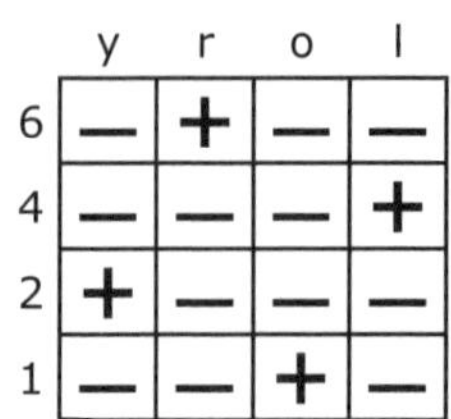

	y	r	o	l
6	—	+	—	—
4	—	—	—	+
2	+	—	—	—
1	—	—	+	—

Answers: y = 2; r = 6; o = 1; l = 4
Since *y* is greater than 1, but less than 4, *y* must be 2. If *r* does not equal *y* times *y*, *r* is not 4. If *r* does not equal *y* minus 1, *r* cannot be 1. Therefore, *r* must be 6, the only remaining number. If *l* does not equal *y* minus 1, *l* is not 1; therefore, *l* must be 4. *o* is then 1.

Page 15: What did the frog say at the library? Read it! Read it! Read it!

	d	e	g	i
12	—	—	—	+
6	—	+	—	—
4	+	—	—	—
2	—	—	+	—

Answers: d = 4; e = 6; g = 2; i = 12
If *e* times *d* equals *i* plus the number of months per year, and *d* does not equal 6, then *e* must be 6, *d* must be 4, and *i* must be 12 for the equation to be true. *g* is then 2.

	r	t	h	b
11	—	+	—	—
7	+	—	—	—
3	—	—	—	+
1	—	—	+	—

Answers: r = 7; t = 11; h = 1; b = 3
If *r* divided by *h* equals *r*, *h* must be 1 for the equation to be true. If *t* plus *r* equals *h* plus 17, and *t* is greater than *r*, *t* must be 11 and *r* must be 7, for the equation to be true. *b* is then 3.

	a	l	f	o
10	+	—	—	—
9	—	—	+	—
8	—	+	—	—
5	—	—	—	+

Answers: a= 10; l = 8; f = 9; o =5
Since *f* plus *f* plus *f* plus *a* equals 37, *f* must be 9 and *a* must be 10, for the equation to be true. If *l* does not equal 5, *l* must be 8, the only remaining number. *o* is then 5.

Page 16: Why aren't fish good tennis players? They don't like getting close to the net!

	n	t	a	l
1	—	—	+	—
2	+	—	—	—
6	—	—	—	+
7	—	+	—	—

Answers: n = 2; t = 7; a = 1; l = 6
If *t* minus *n* equals *n* plus 3, *t* must be 7 and *n* must be 2, for the equation to be true. Since *l* is greater than 3 minus *n*, *l* must be 6, for the equation to be true. *a* is then 1.

	o	f	i	d
4	—	—	+	—
5	—	+	—	—
8	—	—	—	+
9	+	—	—	—

Answers: o = 9; f = 5; i = 4; d = 8
If *o* times 4 equals 36, *o* must be 9 for the equation to be true. Since *i* is less than *o* minus 3, *i* must be either 4 or 5 for the statement to be true. If *f* minus 2 equals 3, *f* must be 5 for the equation to be true. Therefore, *i* must be 4. *d* is then 8.

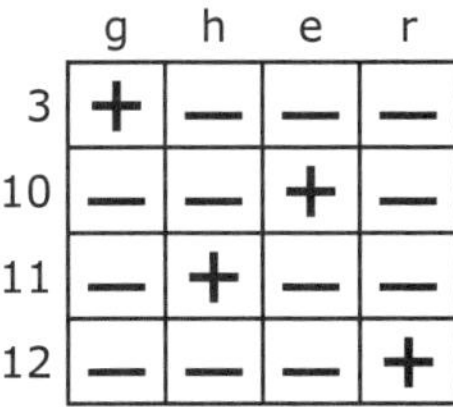

	g	h	e	r
3	+	—	—	—
10	—	—	+	—
11	—	+	—	—
12	—	—	—	+

Answers: g = 3; h = 11; e = 10; r = 12
If *e* plus *g*, minus 2, equals *r* minus 1, *e* and *g* must be either 3 or 10, and *r* must be 12, for the equation to be true. Since *g* plus 8 equals *h*, *h* must be 11 and *g* must be 3 for the equation to be true. Therefore, *e* must be 10.

Page 17: Why did the teacher wear sunglasses in class? Because her class was so bright!

	l	r	h	c
2	—	—	+	—
5	+	—	—	—
8	—	—	—	+
11	—	+	—	—

Answers: l = 5; r = 11; h = 2; c = 8
If *r* times *h* equals 22, *r* and *h* must be either 2 or 11. Therefore, *c* and *l* must be either 5 or 8, and since *c* is greater than *l*, *c* must be 8, and *l* must be 5. If *h* is less than *l*, *h* must be 2. *r* is then 11.

	s	b	g	u
3	+	—	—	—
6	—	—	+	—
9	—	+	—	—
12	—	—	—	+

Answers: s = 3; b = 9; g = 6; u = 12
If *g* equals *s* plus *s*, and *g* is less than 11, *g* must be 6, and *s* must be 3 for the equation to be true. If *b* equals *u* minus *s*, *b* must be 9, and *u* must be 12 for the equation to be true.

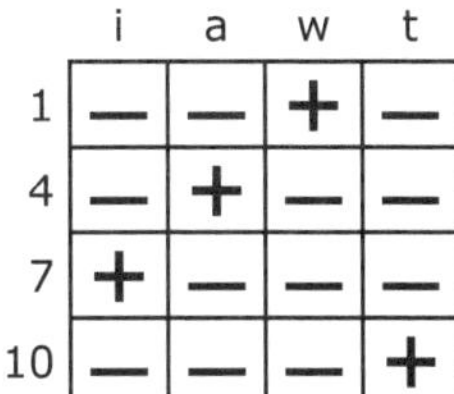

	i	a	w	t
1	—	—	+	—
4	—	+	—	—
7	+	—	—	—
10	—	—	—	+

Answers: i = 7; a = 4; w = 1; t = 10
If *t* minus 3 equals 24 minus 17, *t* must be 10 for the equation to be true. Since *w* equals *a* plus *a* plus 1, minus 8, *w* must be 1, and *a* must be 4 for the equation to be true. *i* is then 7.

Page 18: What kind of shoes do spies wear? Sneakers!

	n	r	t	k
6	—	—	+	—
10	—	—	—	+
8	+	—	—	—
12	—	+	—	—

Answers: n = 8; r = 12; t = 6; k = 10
If *r* is greater than or equal to 12, *r* must be 12 since 12 is the greatest number. If *n* plus *k* equals 18, and *n* is not 6, and *r* is 12, then *n* and *k* must be either 8 or 10 for the equation to be true. Therefore, *t* must be 6, the only remaining number. If *n* plus *n* equals *k* plus *t*, *n* must be 8 and *k* must be 10 for the equation to be true.

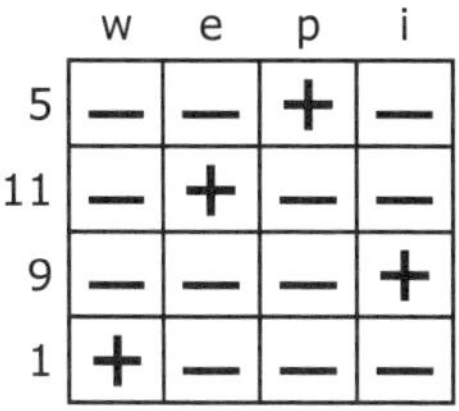

	w	e	p	i
5	—	—	+	—
11	—	+	—	—
9	—	—	—	+
1	+	—	—	—

Answers: w = 1; e = 11; p = 5; i = 9
If *w* is less than or equal to 5, *w* must be either 1 or 5. Since *p* plus *i* equals 14, *p* and *i* must be 5 and 9; therefore, *w* is 1. *p* is less than *i*; therefore, *p* is 5 and *i* is 9. e is then 11.

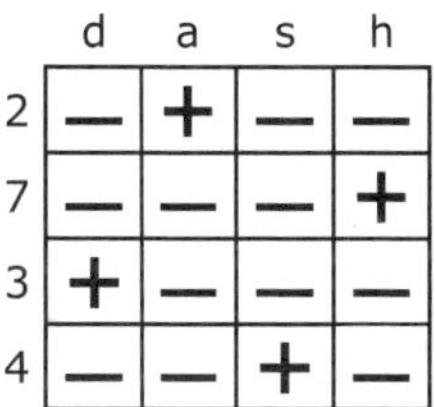

	d	a	s	h
2	—	+	—	—
7	—	—	—	+
3	+	—	—	—
4	—	—	+	—

Answers: d = 3; a = 2; s = 4; h = 7
Since *a* is less than 3, *a* must be 2, the smallest number. Since *d* is less than 4, *d* must be 3. If *s* is less than or equal to *a* plus *a*, *s* must be 4 for the statement to be true. *h* is then 7.

Page 19: What did one flag say to the other flag? Nothing, it just waved!

	v	h	n	g
5	—	—	—	+
10	—	+	—	—
2	+	—	—	—
6	—	—	+	—

Answers: v = 2; h = 10; n = 6; g = 5
If *n* times *n* minus 13 equals *v* plus *h* plus *n* plus *g*, *n* must be 6 for the equation to be true. If *g* plus *g* equals *h* minus *g*, *g* must be 5 and *h* must be 10 for the equation to be true. *v* is then 2.

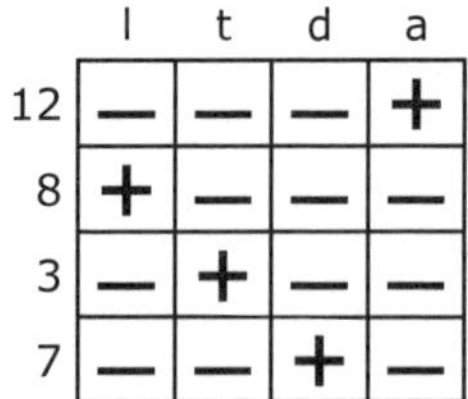

	l	t	d	a
12	—	—	—	+
8	+	—	—	—
3	—	+	—	—
7	—	—	+	—

Answers: l = 8; t = 3; d = 7; a = 12
If *l* is less than 9, but greater than 4, *l* must be either 7 or 8. If *l* plus *a* equals 20, *l* must be 8 and *a* must be 12 for the equation to be true. Since *t* is less than *d*, *t* must be 3, and *d* must be 7.

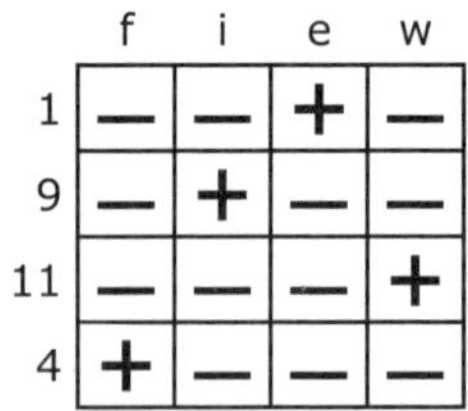

	f	i	e	w
1	—	—	+	—
9	—	+	—	—
11	—	—	—	+
4	+	—	—	—

Answers: f = 4; i = 9; e = 1; w = 11
If *f* is less than *e* plus 5, *f* must be either 1 or 4 for the statement to be true. If *e* plus 10 equals *w*, *e* must be 1 and *w* must be 11 for the equation to be true. Therefore, *f* must be 4. *i* is then 9.

Page 20: Why did the cat go to the computer lab every day? To play with the mouse!

	y	p	m	a
1	—	—	+	—
2	—	+	—	—
5	+	—	—	—
6	—	—	—	+

Answers: y = 5; p = 2; m = 1; a = 6
If *y* does not equal 6, and *y* is greater than *p* plus *m*, *y* must be 5 for the statement to be true with the given numbers. Therefore, *p* and *m* must be either 1 or 2. Since *p* is greater than *m*, *p* must be 2, and *m* must be 1. *a* is then 6.

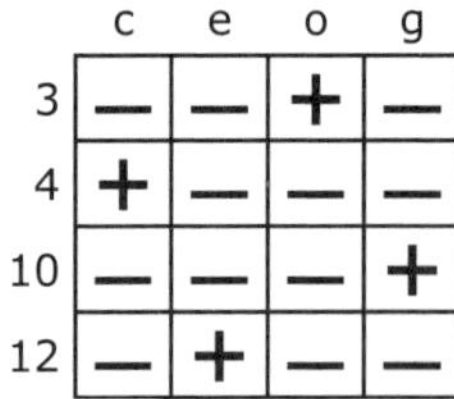

	c	e	o	g
3	—	—	+	—
4	+	—	—	—
10	—	—	—	+
12	—	+	—	—

Answers: c = 4; e = 12; o = 3; g = 10
If *g* times *g*, plus *c*, equals 104, *g* must be 10 and *c* must be 4 for the equation to be true. If *e* minus *c* equals *g* minus 2, *e* must be 12 for the equation to be true. *o* is then 3.

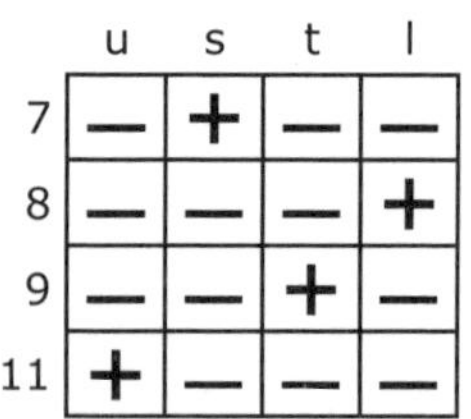

	u	s	t	l
7	—	+	—	—
8	—	—	—	+
9	—	—	+	—
11	+	—	—	—

Answers: u = 11; s = 7; t = 9; l = 8
If *u* minus *s* equals *l* divided by 2, *l* must be 8, the only number divisible by 2 that equals a whole number, *u* must be 11 and *s* must be 7, for the equation to be true. *t* is then 9.

Page 21: Why did the golfer take two pairs of pants to the game? In case he got a hole in one!

	h	c	s	t
10	—	—	—	+
8	+	—	—	—
7	—	+	—	—
5	—	—	+	—

Answers: h = 8; c = 7; s = 5; t = 10
If *t* does not equal 71 minus 63, then *t* is not 8. If *c* is less than 99 minus 91, *c* must be 5 or 7 for the statement to be true. Since *s* is less than *c*, *s* must be 5 and *c* must be 7. Therefore, *t* must be 10 since it is not 8, 5, or 7. *h* is then 8.

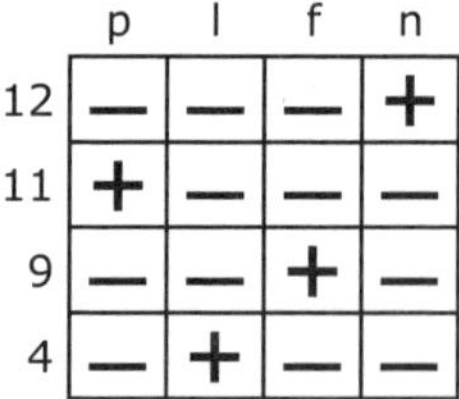

	p	l	f	n
12	—	—	—	+
11	+	—	—	—
9	—	—	+	—
4	—	+	—	—

Answers: p = 11; l = 4; f = 9; n = 12
If *n* is greater than 99 divided by 9, *n* must be 12 for the statement to be true. If *p* does not equal *n* minus 3, *p* is not 9. If *f* does not equal *n* minus 1, *f* is not 11. If *l* is less than *n* divided by 2, *l* must be 4, the only number less than 6. Therefore, *f* must be 9 and *p* must be 11.

	g	o	a	e
6	—	—	+	—
3	—	+	—	—
2	+	—	—	—
1	—	—	—	+

Answers: g = 2; o = 3; a = 6; e = 1
If *a* divided by *o* equals *g*, *a* must be 6, and *o* and *g* must be either 2 or 3 for the equation to be true. Since *e* times *e* equals *g* minus *e*, *g* must be 2 and *e* must be 1 for the equation to be true. Therefore, *o* must be 3.

Page 22: "Waiter, will the pizza be long?" asked the customer. "No sir, it will be round."

	i	g	p	a
1	—	—	+	—
4	+	—	—	—
6	—	—	—	+
11	—	+	—	—

Answers: i = 4; g = 11; p = 1; a = 6
If *p* does not equal 4, and *i* does not equal 1, and *g* minus *p* equals *a* plus *i*, *p* must be 1 and *g* must be 11, and *a* and *i* must be either 4 or 6, for the equation to be true. Since *a* times *p* is greater than *i* times *p*, *a* must be larger than *i*. Therefore, *a* must be 6 and *i* must be 4.

	s	e	z	o
3	+	—	—	—
5	—	+	—	—
8	—	—	—	+
10	—	—	+	—

Answers: s = 3; e = 5; z = 10; o = 8
If *s* plus *z* is less than *e* plus *z*, *s* must be less than *e*. If *z* times *o* equals *s* plus *e*, times *z*, *z* must be 10, *o* must be 8, *s* must be 3, and *e* must be 5 for the equation to be true.

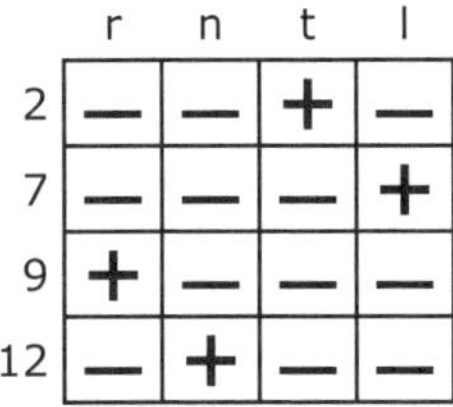

	r	n	t	l
2	—	—	+	—
7	—	—	—	+
9	+	—	—	—
12	—	+	—	—

Answers: r = 9; n = 12; t = 2; l = 7
If *l* times *l* equals 47 plus *t*, *l* must be 7 and *t* must be 2 for the equation to be true. If *r* minus *t* is less than *n* minus *t*, *r* must be less than *n*; therefore, *r* must be 9 and *n* must be 12.

Page 23: What did the picture say to the camera? I've been framed!

	m	t	e	r
4	—	+	—	—
5	—	—	+	—
6	+	—	—	—
8	—	—	—	+

Answers: m = 6; t = 4; e = 5; r = 8
If *m* times *t*, divided by 3, equals *r*, *r* must be 8, and *m* and *t* must be either 4 or 6, for the equation to be true. If *m* divided by 2 is greater than *t* divided by 2, *m* must be greater than *t*; therefore, *m* must be 6 and *t* must be 4. *e* is then 5.

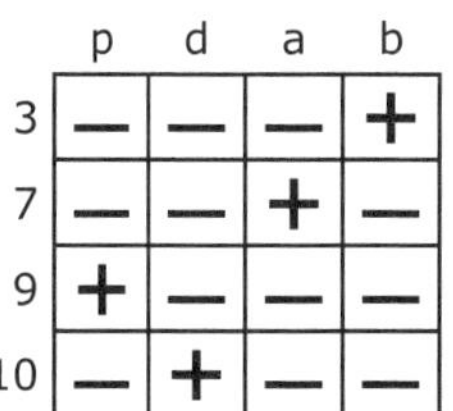

	p	d	a	b
3	—	—	—	+
7	—	—	+	—
9	+	—	—	—
10	—	+	—	—

Answers: p = 9; d = 10; a = 7; b = 3
If *p* is greater than or equal to *b* times *b*, *b* must be 3 and *p* must be either 9 or 10 for the statement to be true. If *d* minus *a* equals *b*, *d* must be 10 and *a* must be 7 for the equation to be true. *p* is then 9.

	f	i	u	c
1	—	—	—	+
2	—	+	—	—
11	+	—	—	—
12	—	—	+	—

Answers: f = 11; i = 2; u = 12; c = 1
If *i* plus 3, times *c*, equals 5, *i* must be 2 and *c* must be 1 for the equation to be true with the given numbers. Since *u* does not equal 10 plus *c*, *u* is not 11; therefore, *u* must be 12. *f* is then 11.

Page 24: What did the salad say to the refrigerator? Close the door; I'm dressing!

	o	g	r	s
2	—	—	—	+
9	—	+	—	—
10	—	—	+	—
11	+	—	—	—

Answers: o = 11; g = 9; r = 10; s = 2
If *s* times 15 equals *o* plus *g* plus *r*, *s* must be 2, and *o*, *g*, and *r* must be 9, 10, or 11. If *o* divided by *s* equals 5.5, *o* must be 11 for the equation to be true. If *r* times *s* is greater than *g* times *s*, *r* must be greater than *g*. Therefore, *r* must be 10 and *g* must be 9.

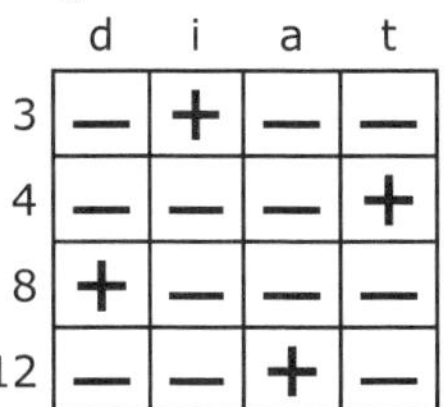

	d	i	a	t
3	—	+	—	—
4	—	—	—	+
8	+	—	—	—
12	—	—	+	—

Answers: d = 8; i = 3; a = 12; t = 4
If *t* equals 2.6 plus 1.4, *t* must be 4. If *i* is less than *t*, *i* must be 3, the smallest number. If *d* does not equal *i* times *t*, *d* is not 12; therefore, *d* must be 8, the only remaining number. *a* is then 12.

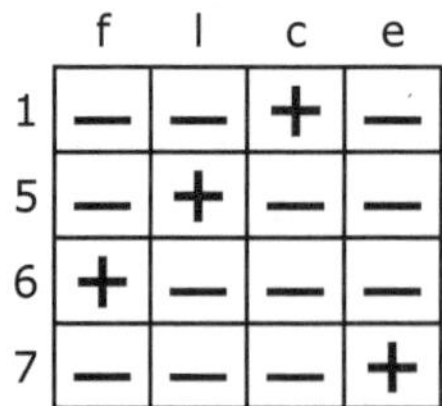

	f	l	c	e
1	—	—	+	—
5	—	+	—	—
6	+	—	—	—
7	—	—	—	+

Answers: f = 6; l = 5; c = 1; e = 7
If *e* divided by 3 does not equal 2, *e* is not 6. If *l* does not equal 4.3 minus 3.3, *l* is not 1. If *l* is less than *f* and *e*, and *l* is not 1, then *l* must be 5, the next lowest number. If *e* is greater than *f* and *l*, and is not 6, *e* must be 7, the largest number. *f* must then be 6 since it is greater than *l* and less than *e*. *c* is then 1.

Page 25: Why was the computer so cold? It forgot to close its windows!

	n	e	i	f
5	—	—	+	—
7	—	+	—	—
9	+	—	—	—
11	—	—	—	+

Answers: n = 9; e = 7; i = 5; f = 11
If *f* is greater than 3.5 plus 5.5, *f* must be 11, the largest number. If *f* minus 3 is greater than *e*, then *e* must be either 5 or 7, and since *e* is greater than *i*, *e* must be 7 and *i* must be 5. *n* is then 9.

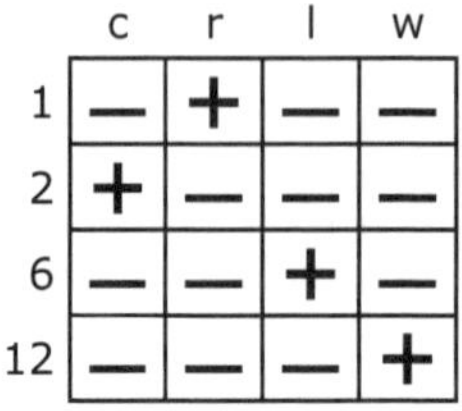

	c	r	l	w
1	—	+	—	—
2	+	—	—	—
6	—	—	+	—
12	—	—	—	+

Answers: c = 2; r = 1; l = 6; w = 12
If *c* divided 4, plus 11.5, equals *w*, *c* must be 2 and *w* must be 12 for the equation to be true. If *r* times *c* is less than *l* times *c*, *r* is less than *l*; therefore, *r* must be 1, and *l* must be 6.

	s	o	d	t
3	—	—	+	—
4	—	—	—	+
8	+	—	—	—
10	—	+	—	—

Answers: s = 8; o = 10; d = 3; t = 4
If *o* is greater than *d* plus *t* plus 1, *o* must be 10, and *d* and *t* must be either 3 or 4, for the statement to be true. If *s* is greater than *d* plus *t*, *s* must be 8, the only remaining number larger than 7. Since *d* is less than *t*, *d* must be 3 and *t* must be 4.

Page 26: What makes music on your head? A head-band!

	w	s	d	u
5	—	—	—	+
2	—	+	—	—
7	+	—	—	—
9	—	—	+	—

Answers: w = 7; s = 2; d = 9; u = 5
If *u* is less than 7, *u* must be either 2 or 5. If *w* minus *s* plus *u* equals 10, *w* must be 7, *s* must be 2, and *u* must be 5, for the equation to be true. *d* is then 9.

	o	m	a	n
6	+	—	—	—
4	—	—	—	+
3	—	+	—	—
10	—	—	+	—

Answers: o = 6; m = 3; a = 10; n = 4
If *m* times *n* equals *o* times 2, *o* must be 6, and *m* and *n* must be either 3 or 4. If *m* times *a* is less than *n* times *a*, *m* must be 3 and *n* must be 4. *a* is then 10.

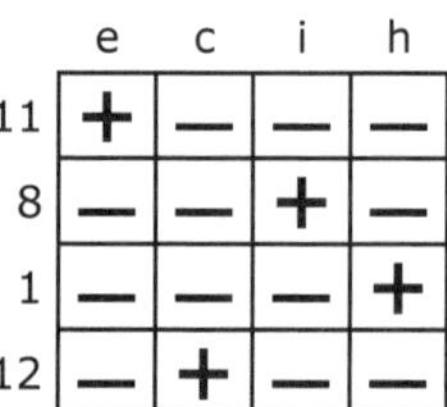

	e	c	i	h
11	+	—	—	—
8	—	—	+	—
1	—	—	—	+
12	—	+	—	—

Answers: e = 11; c = 12; i = 8; h = 1
If *c* times *c* does not equal 64, *c* is not 8. If *e* times *e* does not equal 144, *e* is not 12. If *i* times *h* equals *i*, *h* must be 1. If *h* times *e* does not equal 8, *e* must not be 8, and since it is not 12, *e* must be 11, the only remaining number. Therefore, *c* must be 12. *i* is then 8.

Page 27: What kind of music do mummies like? Wrap!

	a	e	u	i
12	—	—	+	—
10	—	+	—	—
8	+	—	—	—
3	—	—	—	+

Answers: a = 8; e = 10; u = 12; i = 3
If *u* is greater than or equal to 11, *u* must be 12, since 11 is not a given number. If *a* is greater than *i*, but less than *e*, *a* must 8, a middle number. If *i* is less than *a*, *i* must be 3, the lowest given number. *e* is then 10.

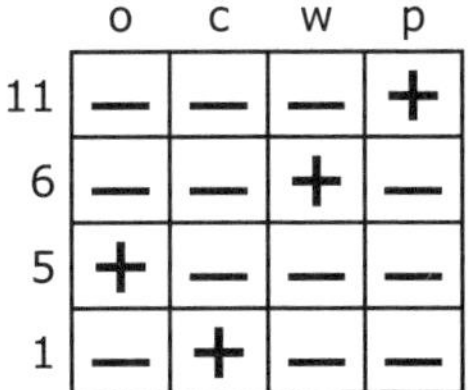

Answers: o = 5; c = 1; w = 6; p = 11
If *o* plus *w* equals *p*, and *o* is greater than 1, and *w* is greater than 5, *o* must be 5, *w* must be 6, and *p* must be 11 for the equation to be true. *c* is then 1.

	s	m	k	r
9	+	—	—	—
7	—	+	—	—
4	—	—	—	+
2	—	—	+	—

Answers: s = 9; m = 7; k = 2; r = 4
If *m* times *s* equals 61 plus *k*, *k* must be 2, and *m* and *s* must be either 7 or 9 for the equation to be true. If *m* divided by *r* is less than *s* divided by *r*, *m* is less than *s*, therefore, *m* must be 7, and *s* must be 9. *r* is then 4.

Page 28: Why did the obtuse angle go to the beach? Because it was over 90 degrees!

	d	s	b	o
12	+	—	—	—
9	—	—	+	—
8	—	+	—	—
3	—	—	—	+

Answers: d = 12; s = 8; b = 9; o = 3
If 10% of 200 equals *d* plus *s*, *d* and *s* must be either 8 or 12 for the equation to be true. Since *d* is greater than 9, *d* must be 12, therefore, *s* must be 8. Since *b* is greater than *s*, *b* must be 9. *o* is then 3.

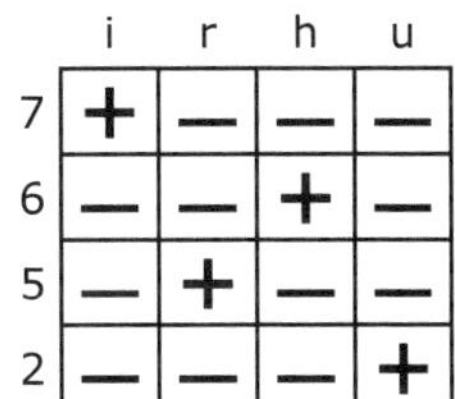

Answers: i = 7; r = 5; h = 6; u = 2
If *h* plus *u* times 100 equals 800, *h* and *u* must be either 2 or 6 for the equation to be true. If *i* times *r* times *r* equals 175, *i* must be 7 and *r* must be 5 for the equation to be true. Since *u* is less than *r*, *u* must be 2, the smallest number. *h* is then 6.

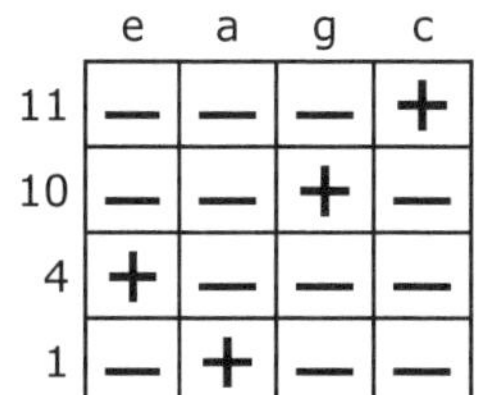

Answers: e = 4; a = 1; g = 10; c = 11
If *g* times *c* equals 124 minus 14, *g* and *c* must be either 10 or 11 for the equation to be true. Since *g* is less than *c*, *g* must be 10 and *c* must be 11. Since *e* is greater than *a*, *e* must be 4, and *a* must be 1.

Page 29: What do you get when you cross poison oak with a four leaf clover? A rash of good luck!

	s	g	p	l
1	+	—	—	—
3	—	—	—	+
4	—	—	+	—
9	—	+	—	—

Answers: s = 1; g = 9; p = 4; l = 3
If *s* times *g* equals *g*, *s* must be 1 for the equation to be true. If *g* times *s* equals *s* plus *l* plus 5, times *s*, *g* must be 9 and *l* must be 3, for the equation to be true. *p* is then 4.

	c	u	e	r
2	—	+	—	—
5	+	—	—	—
6	—	—	—	+
11	—	—	+	—

Answers: c = 5; u = 2; e = 11; r = 6
If *e* times 10 is greater than 100, *e* must be 11 for the statement to be true. If *r* times *e* is greater than 60, *r* must be 6 for the statement to be true. If *r* times *u* is less than 13, *u* must be 2, for the statement to be true. *c* is then 5.

	k	i	o	a
7	—	—	+	—
8	+	—	—	—
10	—	—	—	+
12	—	+	—	—

Answers: k = 8; i = 12; o = 7; a = 10
If *i* divided by *k* equals 1.5, *i* must be 12 and *k* must be 8 for the equation to be true with the given numbers. If *o* times 100 equals *a* times 70, *o* must be 7 and *a* must be 10 for the equation to be true.

Page 30: Why did the orange go to the doctor? He was not peeling well!

	e	n	a	w
12	+	–	–	–
4	–	–	–	+
3	–	–	+	–
2	–	+	–	–

Answers: e = 12; n = 2; a = 3; w = 4
If *a* divided by *w*, plus 2.25 equals *a*, *a* must be 3 and *w* must be 4 for the equation to be true. Since *e* times *a* is greater than *n* times *a*, *e* must be greater than *n*; therefore, *e* must be 12, and *n* must be 2.

	t	g	d	i
11	–	–	–	+
9	–	+	–	–
8	+	–	–	–
7	–	–	+	–

Answers: t = 8; g = 9; d = 7; i = 11
If *i* minus 2, times *g*, equals 81, *i* must be 11 and *g* must be 9 for the equation to be true. Since *d* is less than or equal to 7, *d* must be 7, since 7 is the lowest number. *t* is then 8.

	p	r	c	o
10	–	–	+	–
6	–	–	–	+
5	+	–	–	–
1	–	+	–	–

Answers: p = 5; r = 1; c = 10; o = 6
If *r* times 300 equals *p* times *c* times *o*, *r* must be 1, and *p*, *c*, and *o* must be 5, 6, or 10. If *c* divided by *p* equals *r* plus *r*, *c* must be 10 and *p* must be 5 for the equation to be true. *o* is then 6.